Legends!

A Play

by James Kirkwood

A SAMUEL FRENCH ACTING EDITION

FOUNDED 1830
New York Hollywood London Toronto
SAMUELFRENCH.COM

Copyright © 1983, 1987 by James Kirkwood

ALL RIGHTS RESERVED

CAUTION: Professionals and amateurs are hereby warned that *LEGENDS!* is subject to a Licensing Fee. It is fully protected under the copyright laws of the United States of America, the British Commonwealth, including Canada, and all other countries of the Copyright Union. All rights, including professional, amateur, motion picture, recitation, lecturing, public reading, radio broadcasting, television and the rights of translation into foreign languages are strictly reserved. In its present form the play is dedicated to the reading public only.

The amateur live stage performance rights to *LEGENDS!* are controlled exclusively by Samuel French, Inc., and licensing arrangements and performance licenses must be secured well in advance of presentation. PLEASE NOTE that amateur Licensing Fees are set upon application in accordance with your producing circumstances. When applying for a licensing quotation and a performance license please give us the number of performances intended, dates of production, your seating capacity and admission fee. Licensing Fees are payable one week before the opening performance of the play to Samuel French, Inc., at 45 W. 25th Street, New York, NY 10010.

Licensing Fee of the required amount must be paid whether the play is presented for charity or gain and whether or not admission is charged.

Stock licensing fees quoted upon application to Samuel French, Inc.

For all other rights than those stipulated above, apply to: William Morris Endeavor Entertainment, 1325 Avenue of the Americas, New York, NY 10019.

Particular emphasis is laid on the question of amateur or professional readings, permission and terms for which must be secured in writing from Samuel French, Inc.

Copying from this book in whole or in part is strictly forbidden by law, and the right of performance is not transferable.

Whenever the play is produced the following notice must appear on all programs, printing and advertising for the play: "Produced by special arrangement with Samuel French, Inc."

Due authorship credit must be given on all programs, printing and advertising for the play.

No one shall commit or authorize any act or omission by which the copyright of, or the right to copyright, this play may be impaired.
No one shall make any changes in this play for the purpose of production.
Publication of this play does not imply availability for performance. Both amateurs and professionals considering a production are strongly advised in their own interests to apply to Samuel French, Inc., for written permission before starting rehearsals, advertising, or booking a theatre.
No part of this book may be reproduced, stored in a retrieval system, or transmitted in any form, by any means, now known or yet to be invented, including mechanical, electronic, photocopying, recording, videotaping, or otherwise, without the prior written permission of the publisher.

ISBN 978-0-573-69044-0   Printed in U.S.A.   #13994

AHMET M. ERTEGUN, KEVIN EGGERS, ROBERT REGESTER for EEE VENTURES LTD.
CHERYL CRAWFORD, PACE THEATRICAL GROUP
in association with CENTER THEATRE GROUP/AHMANSON THEATRE LOS ANGELES

present

MARY CAROL
MARTIN CHANNING

A New Comedy by
JAMES KIRKWOOD

with
GARY BEACH ANNIE-JOE

Scenery Designed by   Costumes Designed by   Lighting Designed by
DOUGLAS W. SCHMIDT FREDDY WITTOP THOMAS SKELTON

Directed by
CLIFFORD WILLIAMS

BILLING AND CREDIT REQUIREMENTS

All producers of LEGENDS! must give credit to the Author in all programs and in all instances in which the title of the Play appears for purposes of advertising, publicizing or otherwise exploiting the Play and/or production. The author's name must appear on a separate line in which no other name appears, immediately following the title of the play, and must appear in size of type not less than fifty percent the size of title type.

SYNOPSIS OF SCENES

The place is New York City. The time is the evening.

ACT ONE

Scene 1: A producer's office — late October afternoon.
Scene 2: A Park Avenue apartment — late afternoon, two weeks later.

ACT TWO

Scene 1: Times Square subway station — same day, early evening.
Scene 2: The apartment — an hour later.

THE SETTINGS

A PRODUCER'S OFFICE
This was, in the original production, a roll-on wagon representing Martin Klemmer's small, seedy office. There is a frosted glass door U.C., a file cabinet U.R., below it a desk, chair and a speaker phone which can be used with a receiver or without. A large poster of his current Off-Broadway hit, *Craps,* adorns the wall S.L. of the door. Other theatrical photographs are scattered about the walls.

A PARK AVENUE APARTMENT
A slanted rectangular view of a tasteful apartment, the entrance foyer is one step up and located U.S. to the L.C. One does not see the front door, which is out of sight, farther S.L. There are three sets of French windows, with drapes pulled back and tied, running from near the foyer

at a slanted angle coming D.R. As one enters the room, to the immediate left is a bookcase, an end table, a fireplace with mantel, and D.L. the door to the bedroom.

C.S., facing front, is a comfortable overstuffed sofa, backed by a table which should be about the same height as the back of the sofa. There is a long, low coffee table in front of the sofa, which is used, at various times, to rest feet on, to stand on and sit on, in the case of the stripper. Sylvia also sits on it. S.L. is a chair and stand-up lamp.

S.R. of the sofa is an easy chair on a swivel base, farther Right, another twin swivel chair with just enough room to walk between. Far D.R. is a flowered chair with a footrest and a twin stand-up lamp to the one Stage left. U. of the three chairs and placed along the Upstage windowed wall is a grand piano, slightly to the right of C.S. S.R. of it, next to the piano bench, is a bar cart with glasses, ice and several bottles on it. A fringed shawl with some autographed photographs and a stand-up mirror covers the flat top of the piano. A large painting of Dorothy Coulter, a society woman painted in her late forties, rests on the wall above the mantel, upon which rests a metal crucifix.

The view out of the windows is of other apartment buildings in the distance, not too close. In Act I, the lighting is of late fall afternoon. In Act II, night has fallen and the lamps are on in the apartment and only the lights of other buildings can be seen, not so much the buildings themselves.

Overall, it's an ecletcic, handsome, traditional place, nothing of the mod, high-tech about it. The only change in years has probably been a paint job.

TIMES SQUARE SUBWAY STATION
Small section, the same size as the producer's office in

the first scene. The back wall should be tiled. A three-sided bank of pay phones, push-button style, takes up C.S. The bank of phones has a ledge at about elbow height upon which to place things. There is a wastebasket with various papers and a broken umbrella sticking out of it, S.L., a sign above saying TIMES SQUARE SUBWAY STATION, an exit sign pointing to O.R. The subway tracks would be running parallel to the proscenium — in other words, they would be where the orchestra pit is in relationship to the stage.

CAST OF CHARACTERS

SYLVIA GLENN — Attractive, flashy, former movie star, now around sixty. Still lots of pep and sass. Ambitious to reactivate her career, many times married, but now broke. Beneath the rather shiny veneer, there is a warm woman, who shows herself when she feels secure. In films she usually played the strong, pushy type, like Crawford. She hardly ever played "a lady of breeding." She and Aretha have a special relationship, which allows them to put each other "on" without any hurt feelings.

LEATRICE MONSÉE — (Pronounced Mon-say) Leatrice is around the same age, give or take a few years, as Sylvia. She is a far different kind of movie star, one who always played nuns, nurses and saints. Her public figure was always one of "goodness," but beneath the surface, she was just as strong as Sylvia. A Loretta Young or Joan Fontaine type, with a reputation for sweetness, but underneath lurked what came to be known as "an iron butterfly."

ARETHA THOMAS — A zoftig, black lady with a good sense of humor. She can take kidding and dish it out.

MARTIN KLEMMER — A young, energetic, extremely ambitious producer who has one hit Off-Broadway. A real hustler, he is attractive and uses whatever wiles he has to get ahead.

BOOM-BOOM JOHNSON — A young, very attractive, lithe, black man who strips for women at Chippendale's Club. He also works private parties. His stripping and dancing are done with great style and an open innocence — never a touch of the smarmy. Loves his work, loves to entertain others.

A POLICEMAN — Nice-looking cop in his mid-thirties. Honest, straightforward, not overly bright, but not dumb either.

VARIOUS TELEPHONE VOICES

AUTHOR'S NOTES

Brief notes. The original production toured for over a year with Mary Martin and Carol Channing. Because they were musical comedy stars, the ending was slightly different from the one printed in this version. Toward the end, after they decide to work together, they began reminiscing about a picture they'd done together in which they sang a song. The song we used was "Accentuate The Positive." It began a cappella, then follow spots hit them, a full orchestration was heard and the two ladies sang and danced, excellently choreographed by Peter Gennaro, leading to the final curtain.

The audience loved it, standing ovations every performance, because they wanted to see that part of those talented ladies and they were satisfied. This current ending, I believe, is more legitimate. Also, one does not imagine two musical comedy stars doing this play whenever and wherever it might be done.

The strip number is extremely important and was beautifully choreographed by Trish Garland. Regardless of the breakaway outfit, the bumping and grinding, the working down to a very small gold-tasseled posing strap — the number should be done with a big smile, with joy and innocence. The sexuality is implicit, it should not be played with a smirk.

There are several references that might have to be changed if the play is done in places where there are no K-Marts. A possible change to "Supermarket openings" might do. When there is a mention of *The Enquirer*, if that is not known, the name of any popular scandal sheet can be substituted.

The two ladies are truly adversaries at the beginning of

the play. It is sometimes tempting for two actresses to — for the sake of helping each other — become friendly too soon. The play works much better if the first act is played with as much venom, good-natured and not so good-natured in places, as possible. They are also playing out their well-publicized feud and enjoying it, although each has traits that truly annoy the other. Then, in the second act, when they really let their hair down, there is someplace for the play and the actresses to go.

The relationship between Sylvia and Aretha should never be thought of as even tinged with racism. Anyone who thinks that is, to my mind, just plain stupid. These two know each other, love each other, and this allows them to tease and put each other on. Sylvia is extremely fond of shocking Leatrice and sometimes speaks to Aretha in an outrageous manner for that purpose only. Aretha understands this.

The part of Martin Klemmer, originally and inventively played by Gary Beach, was a comic gem. In casting, this part should be given to the most comedic actor within shouting distance.

In closing, I would like to express my deepest thanks to the crew of the play, who spent a grueling year touring and were always filled with good humor. Also, without the incredible assistance of Keith Baumgartner, we would never have opened in Dallas, nor would we have continued. And a special round of applause must go to Randy Buck, who was our production stage manager and who managed to keep the play together, come hell or high water, both of which, at one time or another, came. Not an easy job, but beautifully done.

The play is an entertainment. But always remember, the audience should empathize with the two ladies and root for them to pull themselves together and do what they know how to do best — put on a show.

The *Legends!* Company
First Performance — January 7, 1986 (Dallas, Texas)
Final Performance — January 18, 1987 (Palm Beach, Florida)

Itinerary	*Miles*
Dallas, Texas: 1/07/86 – 1/18/86 (from Los Angeles)	1425
Los Angeles, California: 1/23/86 – 3/29/86	1425
New Orleans, Louisiana: 4/02/86 – 4/13/86	1921
San Antonio, Texas: 4/15/86 – 4/20/86	564
San Francisco, California: 4/23/86 – 6/01/86	1777
San Diego, California: 6/04/86 – 6/08/86	524
Phoenix, Arizona: 6/11/86 – 6/15/86	800
Sacramento, California: 6/18/86 – 6/22/86	782
Portland, Oregon: 6/25/86 – 7/02/86	587
Seattle, Washington: 7/05/86 – 7/13/86	178
Kansas City, Missouri: 7/16/86 – 7/20/86	1909
Boston, Massachusetts: 7/23/86 – 8/09/86	1427
Washington, D.C.: 8/12/86 – 8/31/86	440
Philadelphia, Pennsylvania: 9/03/86 – 9/28/86	140
Cleveland, Ohio: 10/01/86 – 10/05/86	432
Chicago, Illinois: 10/08/86 – 10/26/86	344
St. Louis, Missouri: 10/29/86 – 11/09/86	293
Atlanta, Georgia: 11/12/86 – 11/16/86	566
Orlando, Florida: 11/19/86 – 11/23/86	451
St. Petersburg, Florida: 11/26/86 – 11/30/86	84
Miami Beach, Florida: 12/03/86 – 12/14/86	248
Fort Lauderdale, Florida: 12/17/86 – 1/04/87	30
Palm Beach, Florida: 1/06/87 – 1/18/87	40
	16,387

Legends!

ACT ONE

Scene 1

A roll-on wagon in front of a curtain graffitied with show business terms: names, plays, etc. The wagon itself represents a section of a grubby theatrical office: cluttered desk, chair, a phone, scripts.
MARTIN KLEMMER, young, energetic, handsome producer in his early thirties talks on the phone.

MARTIN. (*on phone*)—So, Mr. Newman. I still can't believe I'm talking to Paul Newman. So, Mr. Newman, this is what I thought. Wouldn't it be fantastic to get Leatrice Monsée and Sylvia Glenn on the same stage together?

PAUL NEWMAN VOICE. (*laughing*) Leatrice Monsée and Sylvia Glenn—on the same stage? How would you manage that? In cages?

MARTIN. The name Paul Newman alone would get them in a cage, let alone this wonderful new play I've found.

PAUL NEWMAN VOICE. Oops. Hey, sorry—they're calling me on the set. Have to go. Nice talking to you.

MARTIN. But if I could, then you'd be interested in—

PAUL NEWMAN VOICE. Interested . . . Yes. But I doubt it's possible.

MARTIN. I'll be in touch. By the way, how are things out there in the wilds of northern Michigan?

PAUL NEWMAN VOICE. Bleak. I'm surprised you could reach me up here on location.

MARTIN. Where there's a will there's a way. Give my love to Joanne.
PAUL NEWMAN VOICE. Oh, you know Joanne?
MARTIN. Ah—sure, we go way back to . . . Look, I'll talk to you after I nail down Leatrice and Sylvia. Goodbye.
PAUL NEWMAN VOICE. Goodbye. Oh—good luck!
MARTIN. Have a nice day. (*thinks a moment, dials a number*)
WOMAN VOICE. (*on phone*) Shubert Organization.
MARTIN. Bernie Jacobs, please.
WOMAN VOICE. I'm sorry, I don't know if Mr. Jacobs is in. Who's calling?
MARTIN. Paul Newman.
MR. JACOBS VOICE. (*immediately*) Paul—how are you?
MARTIN. Mr. Jacobs, this is Martin Klemmer, producer of the Off-Broadway hit, *Craps!* Your secretary must have gotten her signals slightly confused. Paul asked me to call you. He's found a first play by a young writer. Four characters, one set and he wants to do it, providing he can find the right two actresses to co-star with. Now, if he does, he wondered if you might be interested in booking it into one of your theaters.
MR. JACOBS VOICE. Well, I don't know, I'd have to read the play first.
MARTIN. Yeah?
MR. JACOBS VOICE. And then I'd like to let you know.
MARTIN. The reason I'm calling. Well, you know how the theatrical community is. The Nederlander Organization somehow got wind of Paul's enthusiasm and—
MR. JACOBS VOICE. The Nederlanders?
MARTIN. Yes.
MR. JACOBS VOICE. Well, if Paul's all that

sold . . . We'd be interested. And if we're interested we might invest or we might give you a theater.

MARTIN. Fine, can I tell Paul that's a firm offer?

MR. JACOBS VOICE. I'd like to talk to Paul. Are he and Joanne in Connecticut?

MARTIN. No . . . Ah, Paul's shooting a film in northern — *Sumatra*. But I talk to him every — (*beat*) — other day.

MR. JACOBS VOICE. Well, give him my best and send me a copy of the script.

MARTIN. Will do. Glad we'll be doing business. (*hangs up and dials*)

WOMAN VOICE. Hello . . . ?

MARTIN. Hello, Sylvia Glenn?

SYLVIA VOICE. Yes . . . this is Sylvia Glenn.

MARTIN. This is Martin Klemmer. Producer of the Off-Broadway hit *Craps*. I sent over a script a week or so ago.

SYLVIA VOICE. Oh, yes. Remind me again, what was it?

MARTIN. *Star Wars — The play*.

SYLVIA VOICE. Yes. But, of course, they'll never let you use the title.

MARTIN. Perhaps not, but you read it?

SYLVIA VOICE. Yes.

MARTIN. And did you find it appealing?

SYLVIA VOICE. Yes, actually, it's quite well written. It is. I don't know who you'd get for the man and, of course, the other woman.

MARTIN. Well, I know it's a — bizarre idea, but — (*pause*) You know who would really pull them in at the box office?

SYLVIA VOICE. You mean — besides *me*?

MARTIN. Of course — you! But could you imagine the

stampede if we got a really fine actor — now, I'm already talking to Paul Newman. And —

SYLVIA VOICE. Paul Newman?

MARTIN. Yes, and mind you — this was his suggestion. Now, I know it seems improbable, but Paul thought — you and Leatrice Monsée!

SYLVIA VOICE. Who is this? Larry, is that you? Now, what kind of joke is this?

MARTIN. This is no joke, this is Martin Klemmer, producer of —

SYLVIA VOICE. No joke! Didn't you say Leatrice Monsée?

MARTIN. Well, yes, I did, but —

SYLVIA VOICE. Leatrice Monsée! Well, if that's not a joke . . . (*The laugh turns into a cackle, segueing to a deep belly laugh, followed by a "click" and a disconnect buzz — SYLVIA has hung up. MARTIN hangs up, sighs, consults his pad and dials again.*)

WOMAN VOICE. Hello . . . ?

MARTIN. Hello, may I please speak to Leatrice Monsée?

LEATRICE VOICE. (*This voice is somewhat sweeter than SYLVIA's.*) This is Leatrice Monsée.

MARTIN. This is Martin Klemmer, producer of the Off-Broadway hit *Craps!* I sent you a script a week or so ago.

LEATRICE VOICE. Oh, yes . . . yes, I think I remember. I get so many —

MARTIN. *Star Wars — The Play*!

LEATRICE VOICE. Oh, yes. I remember now. What a delicious title.

MARTIN. What did you think of it?

LEATRICE VOICE. Well, I'm really not that interested in working on Broadway right now. I don't suppose anyone is, what with the cost and the —

MARTIN. Paul Newman is.
LEATRICE VOICE. (*after a beat*) Paul Newman?
MARTIN. Yes, actually it was at his suggestion that I sent the script to you.
LEATRICE VOICE. It was? I hardly know Mr. New— Paul. Oh, we've met several times, of course, but we've never worked together.
MARTIN. Well, undoubtedly he's trying to rectify that. Because, oh boy! he is a great big fan of yours. See, he wants to do the play, but only if he can get two—well, I suppose what you'd call *legends* to play the women.
LEATRICE VOICE. Legends?
MARTIN. Yes. For instance and—well, this was his suggestion. I know how you feel about each other, but Paul thought: you and Sylvia Glenn. (*long silence*)
LEATRICE VOICE. Sylvia Glenn?
MARTIN. Yes. . . .
LEATRICE VOICE. I thought she was in the Smithsonian! (*She hangs up.*)
MARTIN. (*sighs and hangs up*) I'll bet they wouldn't hang up on Paul Newman. (*gets an idea*) No, sir. (*picks up the phone and dials*)
WOMAN VOICE. Hello . . . ?

(*In the following conversation, MARTIN makes his voice skip parts of words and phrases like a bad overseas call.*)

MARTIN. —lo, hello . . . eek to -ylvia -enn, 'ease?
SYLVIA VOICE. Hello? Hello? Who is this?
MARTIN. —ylvia—enn?
SYLVIA VOICE. This is a terrible connection!
MARTIN. This is—aul—ewman . . . —ling!
SYLVIA VOICE. Who?
MARTIN. (*loud and clear*) *Paul Newman.* I'm shooting

a film in—(*As he draws the last word out, he holds the receiver farther away from his mouth.*)—Sumatraaaaaaaaaaaa.

SYLVIA VOICE. Oh, Paul—it's been years. We last met at the Begelmans'. Gladyce was one of my best friends. How's Joanne?

MARTIN. Who?

SYLVIA VOICE. (*Now she's shouting.*) Joanne!!

MARTIN. Oh, she's—ine,—ank you. Look, I was—talking to producer—artin—emmer, and he said that you—ern't too anxious—ork with Miss onsée. Couldn't you please—just—eet with her?

SYLVIA VOICE. Well, I . . .

MARTIN. Oh, it would be great—avor. I think the play's—(*makes raspberry/Bronx cheer sound with his lips*)—and the three of us would be—(*inhales breath, making a loud "eeeek" sound*)—together. Couldn't you just—eet with her?

SYLVIA VOICE. Well, of course, if you want me to just meet with her. I certainly don't want to act like a—well, like she would.

MARTIN. Fine! Sorry . . . (*He bangs the receiver back and forth from the desk to the side of the file cabinet several times.*)—bad connection. I—ways admired and wanted to—ork together! I'll have—producer—artin—emmer set up a—eeting. Really appreciate it, Miss Glenn.

SYLVIA VOICE. Please, Paul, call me Sylvia.

MARTIN. All right, Sylvia. And thank you very—very—(*makes loud hiccuping sound*)—much. 'Bye!

BLACKOUT

END OF ACT I, SCENE, 1

LEGENDS

Scene 2

The curtain rises on the Coulter apartment, decorated with a huge banner that reads "FAREWELL DEAR ARETHA." It stretches from DS.R. *toward the foyer step,* US.L., *at an angle, and is too high to be reached from a standing position. There are clumps of helium balloons, anchored with weights, one resting on the piano and one clump each on the end tables by the sofa. There are other party decorations.*

ARETHA, dressed in a spiffy evening gown, is hurrying around placing streamers and other paper decorations on the lamps as the phone rings.

As she goes to answer it, she passes a fur coat which is draped over the sofa and part of the end table that backs it. The fur slips to the floor, she picks it up, puts it back, but it slips again. She picks it up a second time, slams it down on the back of the sofa.

ARETHA. Stay — or Mama spank! (*picks up the phone, speaks in a formal voice*) Coulter residence. (*as she changes tone*) Oh, hi . . . What — Luther's already on his way over here with the rest of the stuff? . . . Oh, no, that means I'll have to go downstairs and meet him at the delivery entrance . . . Well, child, you know this neighborhood. They give you a ticket for *lookin'* at the building, not to mention parkin' in front of it . . . Catch you later . . . 'Bye! (*hangs up, puts the phone back, grabs the fur coat*) Heel!

(*She goes out the kitchen door. After a second, we hear the front door slam shut. SYLVIA GLENN enters. She carries a clothes bag and a satchel with pictures in it. Shocked by the look of the apartment, she puts her things down.*)

SYLVIA. Hello, is anybody home?—Oh, no! Aretha! Aretha, are you here? (*The phone rings; she answers it in her phone voice.*) Helloooo! Yes, this is Miss Glenn. Yes, *the* Sylvia Glenn. You are? Well, thank you, thank you very much. (*then*) Larry, is that you? Oh, Larry, stop kidding around! I'm so glad you got the message . . . Yes, I'm at Dorothy Coulter's . . . (*glancing around*) Well, the place is decorated like a state fair—or somebody's opened a cat house. Or somebody's opened a cat house *at* a state fair. I don't know but, listen, between 5:30 and 7:00, phone me here, pretend you're calling from the West Coast, you're a producer offering a featured role in a film . . . Well, I don't know, sweetie, you're a writer, use your imagination . . . Well, I'll play anything but Brooke Shield's mother . . . Look, I'm late, I'll explain later. 'Bye. (*Hangs up, looks around. She takes the two clumps of balloons from the end tables into the bedroom. Coming back into the room, she sees the portrait of Dorothy above the fireplace. She takes it down and heads for the bedroom.*) Sorry, Dorothy. I'll have to put you in the closet for a while. Well, think what it did for Dorian Gray. (*She goes into the bedroom. ARETHA comes barreling through the kitchen door with two more clumps of balloons. She stops dead in her tracks as she notices the missing balloons. She looks at her own, then up at the ceiling to see if they've escaped, then back at her own again, and finally shakes her head as if she were mistaken. She sets the new ones down. She looks around and gasps as she notices the missing portrait. She walks to the wall, rubs her hands over the bareness of it to make sure it's not there. She takes her own pulse as she back off; then, suspecting there's a burglar about, she backs fearfully into the kitchen. A beat later, SYLVIA steps out of the bedroom, sees the new balloons, stops, turns to look back into the bedroom to see that the other balloons are still there; they are. Shaking her head in confusion, she quickly grabs the nearest bunch of balloons and carts them off to the bedroom. Just then, ARETHA comes from the kitchen with a huge frying pan. She crosses* US. *of the sofa to* S.L. *as the sound of the balloons popping is heard from the bedroom. ARETHA thinks they're gunshots, crosses herself, steps* DS. *by the mantel, the frying pan held overhead, and as SYLVIA comes striding in from the bedroom, ARETHA swings the pan, barely missing her. SYLVIA turns around; they both scream out.*) Aretha!

ARETHA. Miss Glenn, I thought you were a burglar.

SYLVIA. Aretha, I thought you were on vacation! (*taking in the dress and fur*) Well, well, just look at you!

ARETHA. (*casually*) Oh, I was just out running a few errands.

SYLVIA. Darling, the frying pan doesn't go with that dress at all. (*starting to pick off paper decorations from the* S.L. *lamp*) Aretha, please — help me to get this place back in order. I can't imagine what happened to it.

ARETHA. Miss Glenn, Mrs. Coulter's in Palm Springs visiting the Annenbergs, and —

SYLVIA. I know, and I'm using the apartment for a few days.

ARETHA. Oh, my God!

SYLVIA. Aretha, I'm just using it, I'm not going to set fire to it.

ARETHA. I know, but my niece and namesake, Aretha Waterson's getting married in two weeks and we're having a surprise party for her tonight — here.

SYLVIA. Ahh! I see. That's why all the . . .

ARETHA. But — you'll probably be going out tonight, anyhow, won't you?

SYLVIA. No, that's the whole point, I have a very important meeting here in about — (*glancing at her watch*) — well, just about twenty minutes.

ARETHA. I'm expecting fifteen people here at eight o'clock.

SYLVIA. Good, then there's still time to call and head them off, isn't there? Look, Aretha, I have a vital summit meeting here with a producer and Leatrice Monsée, they must already be on their way.

ARETHA. Leatrice Monsée! Oh, no! You're not going to make a shambles of this apartment. How come you didn't have the meeting over at your place?

SYLVIA. I've just moved over to the West Side to a fabulous walk-in closet. Aretha, three-quarters of this business is appearances. Look, the producer wants me, Paul Newman and Leatrice Monsée.

ARETHA. Paul Newman? Well, I guess I would like to see you back in action.

SYLVIA. Aretha, would you, would you really?

ARETHA. Of course I would.

SYLVIA. Then, honey, please, put the party off for a night or two, help me to pull this thing off. All right, this is it: Leatrice Monsée thinks I live here.

ARETHA. Oh. Miss Glenn!

SYLVIA. Aretha, I'm in big trouble. I'm inches away from broke. (*ARETHA reacts in disbelief as SYLVIA digs in her satchel for a framed photo.*) I swear to God. I don't have time for details, but I blew a big bundle and now my daughter, Lila. Look, here's her picture.

ARETHA. (*taking it*) Oh, isn't she pretty! I remember you always talking —

SYLVIA. And adorable and three times pregnant and married to a high school teacher in Oregon — so you know what that means. They could use a little help and now I finally have an offer.

ARETHA. But I've been planning this party for three weeks and I don't know if I can get a hold of all of them.

SYLVIA. Why, Aretha, does Mrs. Coulter know that you are throwing a party here for your niece?

ARETHA. You know, there was something I forgot to—

SYLVIA. I know Mrs. Coulter and *you* know Mrs. Coulter. And I would not think of mentioning any of this to Mrs. Coulter unless push came to shove. And, sweetheart, welcome to the world of shove.

ARETHA. Well, if it's that important.

SYLVIA. It's that important. I know it's blackmail, but I'm an actress and we're used to doing anything to get our way. (*then sweetly, while hugging her*) Oh, thank you, darling!

ARETHA. (*imitating her sweetness*) You're welcome, dear!

SYLVIA. Oh, and for God's sake, get out of that drag. Leatrice, the nun, will think we've been lunching at Lutece together. (*SYLVIA gets her satchel, walks to the piano and dumps a batch of her pictures on the top as ARETHA dials.*) This place needs more me.

ARETHA. (*on the phone*) Hello, Ella Mae Sue Ella, honey? . . . We've had an emergency catastrophe. Now, you've got that whole party list. Well, call everyone and tell 'em we've been preempted for tonight . . . Yeah, child, we're eighty-sixed, out the window . . . Well, we'll have it—(*to SYLVIA*) How long are we privileged to have your presence amongst us?

SYLVIA. (*setting her pictures up*) Oh, just a couple of days. I'll go to the movies tomorrow, if you want.

ARETHA. No, no . . . (*back on the phone*) Monday night, same time, same station. Oh, and as soon as you reach everyone, phone and let me know. All right, girlfriend, we'll party Monday night . . . Talk to you

later . . . 'Bye. (*hangs up*) Oooo, let me go get out of this outfit.
SYLVIA. Oh, you better bring a ladder. We have to get the rest of this stuff down. And let's get rid of some of this food. (*picks up two plastic-wrapped plates of food from the coffee table*) I don't want Miss Only Perfect Person In The World to think I rigged up a banquet just for her.
ARETHA. (*taking the food*) Gotcha! (*ARETHA exits into the kitchen as SYLVIA hurries to the phone, sits on the sofa and dials.*)
SYLVIA. (*on the phone*) Doris, Sylvia. Got a pen? . . . Good, take this number down: 736-1689 . . . Now, between 5:30 and 7:00, call and invite me to some perfectly fabulous party or dinner or opening or closing or funeral or whatever and drop a few names . . . Huh? . . . What? . . . What? . . . She did? . . . When? . . . Where? . . . In Vermont? . . . Two weeks ago! . . . But that's impossible, we'd have all heard about it . . . Oh, just now! . . . Oh, no! . . . Oh, my Gaa---wd! . . . How dreadful! (*laughing*) That's the most gruesome thing I ever heard! . . . Of course, lunch tomorrow! I want to hear every last gory detail! . . . 'Bye . . . (*hangs up, mutters*) I never did trust cats. (*SYLVIA looks at the mantel, retrieves a vase of flowers on a table us. of it, places them on the mantel to hide the discolored spot left by the portrait's removal, fluffs the flowers out more, sees a crucifix on the mantel, picks it up.*) I know it's not fair to pray only when you need something, but — (*crosses herself*) If you'll only help me to pull this off, I'll go to Mass every Sunday and I'll never get married again. Please. It's mainly for Lila and she's turning out little Catholics like crazy for you. Five in three years! Oh, and tonight, please help me remember my own mother's advice, try to be

popular, try *not* to be yourself. (*She puts the crucifix back as ARETHA appears in the doorway dressed in a maid's outfit. She carries a metal stepladder and places it under the* S.R. *end of the banner.*) Well, well, well, just look at us.

ARETHA. (*a la Prissy*) Watcha want me to do next, Missee Glenn, I done finished birthin' *all* dem babies.

SYLVIA. Frankly, Scarlett, I don't give a damn. Oh, Aretha, you are a doll. I owe you one.

ARETHA. (*climbing the ladder*) Well, how about breakfast in bed tomorrow?

SYLVIA. You're on. I'll make my famous eggs a la Sophie Tucker. (*ARETHA pulls a string, releasing that end of the banner, which SYLVIA catches.*) So yummy and only about five thousand calories.

ARETHA. (*climbing down the ladder, then moving it to the* US.L. *end of the banner and climbing up it again*) Oh, Miss Glenn, you're terrible, just terrible. But I guess that's why I always took to you. Most of Mrs. Coulter's friends are so — well, uppity-tuppity. But you're just terrible. I bet you got some real trash in you!

SYLVIA. Yeah, real trash. (*She starts folding the banner.*) Look, we'll just fold up Aretha, Jr. She'll be as good as new.

ARETHA. You broke? But — one of the biggest movie stars ever!

SYLVIA. And one of the dumbest with a buck. I thought it would never end. Well, it did.

ARETHA. But you have such an exciting life. You know, I always wanted to be an actress. I always wanted to be — Doris Day. I mean, parties and going out on the town, here, there and —

SYLVIA. Nowhere! An exciting life? Do you know the last big event I attended was right here for dinner — that was two weeks ago last Tuesday.

ARETHA. (*releasing the other end of the banner*) But — Sylvia Glenn!

SYLVIA. That's just the curse. "Sylvia Glenn? We wouldn't dare invite her, she's all booked up." Well, Sylvia Glenn is sitting at home watching "Dallas" or "Falcon Crest" or "Dynasty" and wishing to hell someone would ask her to be on one and wondering what witch doctor Joan Collins goes to to keep looking like that!

ARETHA. (*climbing down the ladder*) Well, I read in *The Enquirer* where she eats monkey glands!

SYLVIA. *Takes* monkey glands, Aretha. (*shudders*) They don't eat them.

ARETHA. (*crossing toward the kitchen with the ladder*) Oh, I thought they ate them. Well, that's good to know 'cause I was wondering how they ate them. Deep-fried or boiled or —

SYLVIA. Stop it, Aretha! (*Intercom buzzes.*) Jesus, Mary and Joseph, there they are! (*ARETHA walks to the intercom as SYLVIA goes after the last bunch of balloons with a letter opener she picks up from table backing the sofa.*) She was always early, always standing around in full make-up, ready and waiting before they ever even set up the lights. Damn woman! I'll get you, Leatrice Monsée! (*gets the last two balloons with one thrust*) Ah-hah, got both her heads!

ARETHA. (*at intercom*) Yes . . . send her up, please. Thank you.

SYLVIA. (*as ARETHA hurries to take the step-ladder and remaining party decorations into the kitchen*) Now, when you let them in, think before you speak. Remember, a slip of the lip can sink a ship — don't spill the beans! Now, if she has a drink — slug it! What I wouldn't give to see her crawling around on her hands and knees. And if we get into a fight—you are on my side.

ARETHA. And how, Kimo Sabe!

SYLVIA. I'm going to slip into that divine little tea gown I wore in *That Was No Lady*.

ARETHA. Yeah, I saw you in *That Was No Lady*—and you sure weren't! (*The doorbell rings.*)

SYLVIA. Aretha, wish me luck, I really need for this to work, I really do.

ARETHA. Why sure, honey, sure.

SYLVIA. (*getting her clothes bag*) Thank you!

ARETHA. (*calling out*) Coming!

SYLVIA. If this doesn't work out, I'll be the only female movie star taxi driver in New York City. (*on her way to the bedroom*) I hope she looks like Sam Jaffe in *Gunga Din*! (*Doorbell rings again.*)

ARETHA. Coming! Ooooeeee, we're up to our asses in movie stars! (*ARETHA picks up bits of the balloons that SYLVIA has broken, glances around, stuffs them down the front of her dress, then she hurries to the front door. Offstage:*) Come in.

LEATRICE. (*offstage*) Hello, I'm Leatrice Monsée.

ARETHA. (*offstage*) Oh, you don't have to tell me that. I'm a fan of yours from way back!

LEATRICE. (*offstage*) Oh, how sweet.

ARETHA. (*offstage*) Miss Glenn said there was a gentleman . . .

LEATRICE VOICE. Yes, he'll be along in just a little while.

(*They enter. LEATRICE MONSÉE is the same age, give or take a year, as SYLVIA and dressed fit to kill: gorgeous fur cape, hanging almost down to her ankles, handsome shoes, purse, gloves. She carries a script in a leather-bound folder..)*

ARETHA. My, my, don't you look like you just now stepped off the silver screen.
LEATRICE. Why, thank you. How very dear of you. (*glancing around*) What a lovely apartment.
ARETHA. Yes.
LEATRICE. Sylvia always did have taste in clothes, cars and houses — if nothing else. (*light little laugh*)
ARETHA. Oh, it is so good to finally meet you. Lord, I guess you suffered more than any lady in pictures. And I suffered through each and every one of them right along with you. Remember in *Rainbow's End*, when that mean ole George Saunders had your brains operated on and you went back into being a little baby girl?
LEATRICE. That wasn't very nice of him, was it?
ARETHA. Nice! Um-umn! And in *The Sin of Stephanie Brooks* when your mean old brother-in-law-to-be had you raped so you wouldn't pass the virginity test — so his brother wouldn't marry you!
LEATRICE. (*crossing* S.L.) Robert Mitchum was certainly a meanie in that one.
ARETHA. Well, if you'll excuse the expression — he was mean as catshit! (*LEATRICE gasps.*) Oh, yes, that man was mean! And when you got captured by all those savages in Borneo. And oh, what they didn't do to you, the way they dragged you through that jungle. And by the hair, too. How come your hair didn't come out? And when you were asleep under that tree and that great big old snake —
LEATRICE. (*shudders*) Please — I'm terrified of snakes. They had to use a double.

LEGENDS 29

ARETHA. Sure looked like your belly that snake crawled across.

LEATRICE. Oh — please! Even the word does me in.

ARETHA. But that was one mean batch of little pygmies you ran into, too. You know, they say any breed of thing — when they get that little — is mean! Little ponies — Shetland ponies. They're mean. Little people, too: Hitler, Napoleon, Mickey Rooney — mean. It's just like all the meanness gets crunched up in a tight little ball and there's no room for it to spread around, so they just can't help being plain mean!

LEATRICE. I never thought of that.

ARETHA. It's true. Let me take your cape.

LEATRICE. Will Sylvia be long?

ARETHA. Oh, she'll be right out . . .

LEATRICE. (*fluffing her coat up, crossing* S.R.) Well, I think I'll keep it on for just a little while, I'm still chilly. It's nippy out!

ARETHA. It sure is. Let me get you a drink.

LEATRICE. (*sitting*) Oh, I don't really drink.

ARETHA. Well, some cola or tea? Or some soda with fresh lime?

LEATRICE. Say — fresh lime sounds good. (*as ARETHA heads toward the bar*) Now, let's see, what goes nice with fresh lime?

ARETHA. Well, we have most —

LEATRICE. I know. Gin. Gin-on-the-rocks!

ARETHA. Gin-on-the-rocks?

LEATRICE. It's so cold I'll just have one. Gin-on-the-rocks, but, please, don't make it too strong.

ARETHA. A weak gin-on-the-rocks with a squirt of fresh lime coming up. (*as she makes the drink*) Well, I guess my favorite picture was the one you made with

Miss Glenn. Whoo-ow, you were a pair. The two of you! And when it turned out — you were the psycho.

LEATRICE. For once — they let me win!

ARETHA. Win? They sent you to the electric chair. They shaved your head, and let you spit out all that hatred you hid for so many years as they walked you down that long hall to be fried!

LEATRICE. In Hollywood — that's called winning.

ARETHA. Why the two of you didn't make another picture together, I'll never know.

LEATRICE. (*laughing warmly*) Lloyd's of London refused to insure us.

ARETHA. (*laughing too*) Of course, I know. You two were terrors, weren't you?

LEATRICE. Oh . . .

ARETHA. Yes, you were. 'Fess up. You two were holy terrors. Why, you got all that publicity! I sure wish I'd been workin' for one of you then 'cause I sure would love to get the inside dope on that little caper.

LEATRICE. Surely you've gotten it from Sylvia. At least her side. How long have you been working for her?

ARETHA. Oh — ah, I've been working for her . . . ah, three years. Gee, it seems like I just started.

LEATRICE. Three years. You must have a strong constitution.

ARETHA. Oh, Miss Glenn's bite is not nearly as bad as her bark. She's just real people.

LEATRICE. If she's just "real people" — I wouldn't venture outside the house. Imagine New York City peopled by eight million Sylvia Glenns. Why, the sound of the ambulances alone would be absolutely deafening.

ARETHA. You sure have a way with words, Miss Monsée.

(*SYLVIA, dressed in a backless silver lamé gown, loaded with jewelry, appears in the bedroom doorway. She focuses on LEATRICE. Both are gussied up fit to kill. LEATRICE gives her a long stare—from head to toe.*)

LEATRICE. For a second there . . . I thought it was the Tin Man from *The Wizard of Oz*.
SYLVIA. Well, well, well—just look at us.
LEATRICE. Correct me if I'm wrong—but didn't you used to be Sylvia Glenn? (*They laugh, then speak together.*)
LEATRICE & SYLVIA. I thought you were dead!
SYLVIA. Well, where's Mr. What's-his-name?
LEATRICE. (*standing*) Klemmer, Martin Klemmer. He phoned just as I was going out the door, said he tried to get in touch with you, something about an emergency meeting about the play. He'll be along in just a little while. (*parading and crossing in front of SYLVIA*)
SYLVIA. My, my, my—what a ravishing cape.
LEATRICE. And don't you look simply *marvelous*.
SYLVIA. If it was any longer you could dust the floors. (*catty*) Aretha, better look out for your job! (*She turns toward LEATRICE, holds out her arms.*) C'mere and give us a kiss. (*As LEATRICE looks at her for a long moment, deciding whether or not to accept the offer, ARETHA picks up a small flash camera from the bar area.*)
LEATRICE. (*finally walking toward her*) Well, why not . . . ? (*stops just short*) Ah-ah, no biting! (*They begin to embrace but as they do, LEATRICE sees ARETHA and the camera and pulls back.*) No, no, only from above, get up on a chair or something!
SYLVIA. (*switching sides*) And wait—wait, my right

side! (*ARETHA giggles as she steps up on a chair or ottoman, aims the camera and gets the two of them kissing, although all four eyes are aimed at the camera, plus dazzling stage smiles. There's a flash, they pull apart, the smiles snap shut.*)

ARETHA. (*indicating the camera*) Thank you, I had it for the party. (*realizing she's getting into unwanted territory*) I'll get some canapes. (*She leaves.*)

SYLVIA. There, that wasn't so bad after all, was it?

LEATRICE. (*staring at her*) I simply cannot get over you. You haven't had something—well, *done*, have you?

SYLVIA. Me? Are you mad? I wouldn't let anyone touch me with a knife.

LEATRICE. What are they using now—laser beams?

SYLVIA. Same dear sweet Leatrice.

LEATRICE. Same dear *old* Sylvia.

SYLVIA. All right, enough—enough. Let's make a bargain, let's forget the past.

LEATRICE. Do you really mean that?

SYLVIA. I always mean what I say. (*taking off LEATRICE's cape*) Take off the cape. Seen, registered, you're doing well, looking terrific. Take it off! (*yanks it off and yells to the kitchen*) Aretha, haul it out here!

LEATRICE. Sylvia!

SYLVIA. Oh, we just kid around . . . now look, let's get one thing straight. Everything I say—you're not going to "Sylvia" me. I mean, aren't we past that?

LEATRICE. I suppose so.

SYLVIA. Well, hooray for us.

ARETHA. (*coming in*) You bellowed, madam?

SYLVIA. Yes. Aretha, take this out to the kitchen and singe it!

LEATRICE. (*walks US.L. of the sofa, taking off her hat,*

glancing in a small mirror on the mantel) You haven't changed one single, teensy tiny iota.

SYLVIA. I know, isn't it heaven? (*LEATRICE discovers a framed photo lying on the floor under the table backing the sofa. Puzzled for a moment, she dismisses it as SYLVIA, by the bar, looks into her glass and speaks to ARETHA.*) Aretha, what's in this, soda?

ARETHA. Gin-on-the-rocks.

SYLVIA. Gin-on-the-rocks, eh? Well, there's only so much slugging you can do with that! (*ARETHA exits into kitchen.*) Well, sit down — take your girdle off. Gin-on-the-rocks, eh?

LEATRICE. (*sitting on the sofa*) I'm only having one. Also, I admit, I was a teensy, tiny bit apprehensive about this meeting. I upped my insurance and left a sealed envelope with my lawyer.

SYLVIA. (*sitting beside her*) I love you. Teensy, tiny . . . that's one thing I never understood about you. One of the most ruthless characters in Hollywood — and that's saying something.

LEATRICE. (*immediate protest*) Oh —

SYLVIA. Come on, this is Sylvia you're talking to. Sylvia Glenn, star of stage, screen and —

LEATRICE. — K-Mart openings!

SYLVIA. Now, that's what I mean about you. You've always had a wicked sense of humor, you can see it right behind the eyeballs. It was always visible to me. But, of course, you'd never swear or really drink, or —

LEATRICE. Oh, all that's changed.

SYLVIA. When?

LEATRICE. In recent years.

SYLVIA. I don't believe it. Prove it.

LEATRICE. No.

SYLVIA. I don't believe it anyway. I remember that

swear box you used to keep on the set. Anybody'd swear and they had to drop in a quarter. (*laughing*) And Ethel Merman came up to you once and said, "I hear it costs a quarter every time you say a no-no. Well, babe, here's five bucks, go fuck yourself!"

LEATRICE. (*shocked*) How can you say that about dear, sweet Ethel?

SYLVIA. Easy. Well, I think we're going to get along just dandy. Oh, come on, let's dish before Mr. What's-his-name gets here.

LEATRICE. Shouldn't we read through the script first?

SYLVIA. We're not going to read for him, we don't have to audition, do we?

LEATRICE. Well, no, but—

SYLVIA. Come on, let's talk, we can't meet after all these years and start whipping through a script right off the bat. (*then*) Oh—of course, of course. I almost forgot! Did you hear about Maggie Bain?

LEATRICE. (*suddenly eager*) No—what's she done now?

SYLVIA. She bought the farm.

LEATRICE. I know, the old witch bought a farm up in Vermont. Oh, those poor cows and horses!

SYLVIA. No, no, I was using the phrase in its metaphorical sense. She croaked.

LEATRICE. Croaked?

SYLVIA. Croaked. Talked to Doris Tilton, not a half hour ago. Maggie has gone to her reward, which should be quite amusing—if fair's fair.

LEATRICE. Oh, dear, I didn't mean to call her an old witch.

SYLVIA. Oh, come off it, Leatrice—they don't change just because they're dead, you know.

LEATRICE. Sylvia!

LEGENDS 35

SYLVIA. Well, they don't. But the best part, the absolute juiciest — you remember all those cats she had?

LEATRICE. Yes, nobody else would put up with her.

SYLVIA. Well, get this. Apparently she had a heart attack and died all alone during that terrible blizzard we had two weeks ago. No one came by, they couldn't, see, the people who phoned thought she'd gotten out. But she didn't and the cats didn't either. They ran out of dried cat food and whatever else they could dig up and by the time somebody found Maggie — the cats had started to eat her!

LEATRICE. They didn't!

SYLVIA. They did!

LEATRICE. (*hands to face, shuddering*) Oh, how gruesome, how Edgar Allan Poe!

SYLVIA. (*a put-on, reaching for the script*) Yes. Well, now — let's have a look at that script and —

LEATRICE. Wait a minute, wait a minute!

SYLVIA. Yes, what?

LEATRICE. (*conspiratorily*) How much of her did they eat?

SYLVIA. I don't know, but those must have been some hungry cats.

LEATRICE. Strong teeth, too.

SYLVIA. She was a tough broad.

LEATRICE. I'd have started in on the furniture first.

SYLVIA. Please pass the desk! (*They both laugh, then:*)

LEATRICE & SYLVIA. Poor Maggie.

SYLVIA. (*standing, crossing to the bar*) Oh, come on, I'll make you a drink. Let's talk.

LEATRICE. The cats ate Maggie Bain!

SYLVIA. Not all of her. They just didn't find an old shoe and no Maggie. The cats ate *some* of her.

LEATRICE. I wonder which parts they left?

SYLVIA. Leatrice, you are absolutely morbid about this. (*crossing back to the sofa with a drink*)

LEATRICE. Well, you have to admit it doesn't happen every day. My little Muffin wouldn't do a thing like that.

SYLVIA. (*sitting*) Can your little Muffin work a can opener?

LEATRICE. Of course not.

SYLVIA. Then don't put her to the test.

LEATRICE. The cats ate Maggie Bain!

SYLVIA. Well, that's the word. Now, let's change the subject, it could get a little depressing.

LEATRICE. Right, you're absolutely right. You know, I'm beginning to enjoy myself.

SYLVIA. Well, with all this good news.

LEATRICE. It isn't that exactly.

SYLVIA. You always had a weird streak. You tried to hide it, but it was there.

LEATRICE. Maybe just a teensy tiny.

SYLVIA. (*mimicking LEATRICE, sweet baby voice*) Maybe. About the size of Argentina.

LEATRICE. (*warning*) Sylvia!

SYLVIA. I don't know why, but I always liked to mimic you.

LEATRICE. I know. And I don't know why, but I never liked it — at all.

SYLVIA. All right. I won't, I won't, I swear.

(*ARETHA enters with canapes.*)

ARETHA. How about some canapes, Miss Monsée?

LEATRICE. (*at her goodiest*) Why, thank you. How very dear of you. (*fingers hovering over tray*) Smoked salmon and caviar. Why, they look like little caviar baskets, don't they?

SYLVIA. *(baby talk)* Yes — ums a liddle caviar basket — just for Lea-trice.

LEATRICE. Sylvia, I wish you wouldn't do that.

SYLVIA. I know, Bad Sylvia! *(slaps her own hand, but continues the baby talk)* Her's a bad dirl!

LEATRICE. *(chewing on her food)* I really wish you wouldn't.

SYLVIA. It's only — I've never gotten over you talking that way through more than half a movie and getting nominated for an Academy Award.

LEATRICE. I was retarded in that movie.

SYLVIA. I hope to *tell* you! And you were perfect.

LEATRICE. You never won an Oscar, did you?

SYLVIA. I did, too. And you know it. I won it in 1968 for playing a hooker in *Go For Broke*.

LEATRICE. Oh, yes. Ah, but . . .

SYLVIA. Yes, it was for Best Supporting Actress.

LEATRICE. Are the supporting ones the same as for Best Actress?

SYLVIA. No, of course not. Mine is made out of cardboard, stuck together with Krazy Glue.

LEATRICE. No need to get testy.

SYLVIA. I'm not testy. *(As ARETHA passes the tray to her, SYLVIA snaps in a loud voice.)* NO! *(recovering)* Thank you. *(back to LEATRICE)* Well, we each won an award. Me for a hooker and you for a nun. Oh, say that last speech for me. Go ahead.

LEATRICE. "You can laugh and bray all you want. You can call me a Bride of Christ, but you can't take away my faith in — "

SYLVIA. No, No, not the nun thing, the one from *Rainbow's End*.

LEATRICE. I don't remember it.

SYLVIA. You do, too. You remember every line you

ever had and lots of everybody else's lines.

LEATRICE. All right, I remember it. But I won't say it.

ARETHA. Oh, I just loved that movie, it was so sad. I cried so, until—my sinuses threw in the towel. Please . . .

LEATRICE. All right, I'll say it for Aretha, but no laughing.

SYLVIA. Of course not.

LEATRICE. (*gets off the sofa, takes a cushion, kneels* DS., *closes her eyes for a second, then opens them*) "Her knows her won't see Donny again. Her knows her would wike her own baby, but her knows her can't . . . can't ever. If only her mind had kept up wif her body, but . . . no—no—(*shakes her head*) So—I think I just go bye-bye now. (*folds her hands together in prayer*) Now I way me down to seep—I pway the Lord my soul to—to—"

SYLVIA. I'll be George Saunders. (*serious*) "To keep, my dear girl—to keep!"

LEATRICE. (*shaking her head*) "no, no—to take. Oh, please dear Lord—to take!"

ARETHA. (*after a moment*) Oh, that's lovely . . . just lovely.

SYLVIA. You were damned good.

LEATRICE. (*sitting on the sofa again*) Then why did you always make fun of me?

SYLVIA. Oh . . . I don't know. You were forever playing nurses and nuns and saints and I was stuck playing tramps.

LEATRICE. That was not my fault. It was type-casting. I never made fun of you when you played all those bitches.

SYLVIA. What's to make fun of a bitch?

LEATRICE. Oh . . . ? (*stands, then puts a knee on the*

sofa, a hand on the back, tough pose, tough voice) "Listen to me, Frank. I'll get to Chi-cagah if I have to get there on a freight train, on a Greyhound bus or on my *back!*"

ARETHA. (*clapping her hands and laughing*) That's it, that's her. And if you'll excuse the expression — she mostly got there on her *back*. (*SYLVIA silences her with a look.*)

LEATRICE. (*to SYLVIA as she crosses to chair,* S.L.) Now you play Kirk Douglas.

SYLVIA. Okay, Kirk Douglas. (*stands, plants a foot on the coffee table, speaks toughly, through clenched teeth*) "But what about the kids, Marcy?"

LEATRICE. (*tough again*) "Keep 'em!"

SYLVIA. "Keep 'em? Keep the kids?"

LEATRICE. "All right, don't keep 'em — have a yard sale!" (*ARETHA applauds; so does SYLVIA.*)

SYLVIA. You see, you could have played a perfect bitch if you'd only wanted to.

LEATRICE. (*interest piqued*) Me, play a bitch? Why, I . . .

ARETHA. (*laughing*) I still like the part about you getting to Chicago on your back!

SYLVIA. Aretha, why don't you go out in the kitchen and — *do* something.

ARETHA. Oh, everything's done.

SYLVIA. (*winking at ARETHA, patting her shoulder*) Well, then, dear, why don't you go out and — pick some cotton?

LEATRICE. Sylvia!

SYLVIA. Leatrice!

ARETHA. (*laughing, crossing to LEATRICE*) It's all right, I get a kick out of her. Out of all Mrs. Coulter's friends — (*stops herself, turns and heads for the kitchen*) I think I *will* pick some cotton. (*She leaves.*)

LEATRICE. Who is Mrs. Coulter?

SYLVIA. Oh, a mutual friend. She's who I got Aretha from. Now, whenever she's giving a large dinner party, I lend her Aretha. (*sits on the coffee table, then*) Leatrice, what do you think of the play?

LEATRICE. I think it's sad, funny, heartbreaking . . .

SYLVIA. And just like the business.

LEATRICE. The business! What a funny word for it.

SYLVIA. What a funny business. (*after a moment of reflection*) Do you miss it?

LEATRICE. The business?

SYLVIA. No, our time — at the top of the mountain. Our reign. When we were the — what? The Goddesses. Oh, Leatrice, we were surrounded by the most fascinating, talented people in the world: directors, writers, producers, designers — but, when they yell "cut" they mean cut! When they turn off the spotlight, you feel the chill.

LEATRICE. (*standing, crossing to* C.S.) Of course, I get offered things all the time, but I won't do trash. Like — oh, those awful TV series with —

SYLVIA. Oh, no. You mean "Falcon Crest," "Dynasty," "Dallas."

LEATRICE. Icky, icky, icky.

SYLVIA. Tacky, tacky, tacky. (*They've let their hair down now, lest they go too far.*)

LEATRICE. Thank heavens for wise investments.

SYLVIA. Wise investments? I heard you were — financially fragile.

LEATRICE. Financially fragile? Oh, no . . . I've never lived up to my means. And I've certainly never lived past them — like so many people in our profession. For instance, I don't even keep a car and driver anymore. Sometimes when I want to go to the theater I rent a limo, but most of the time I just hop into a cab!

SYLVIA. Well, next thing you'll be taking the subways.

LEATRICE. (*breathless, sitting on coffee table next to SYLVIA*) I took a subway once, just last year. After that huge snowstorm. I couldn't get a car or driver or anything, so the gent that was taking me to the theatre that night said: "I know, Leatrice, let's take the subway!"

SYLVIA. Say, you always went around with some pretty smart cookies, didn't you?

LEATRICE. Darling, I know when you're putting me on and you're putting me on now and — that's not nice. Financially fragile? Strangely enough, I've heard that about you.

SYLVIA. You did? Who told you that?

LEATRICE. Last summer, Mary Lou Berman said —

SYLVIA. Oh, well, would you take anything Mary Lou Berman said as gospel? Do you realize how old Mary Lou is now?

LEATRICE. She's certainly older than she looks.

SYLVIA. Of course she is. She's even older than she is.

LEATRICE. Well, apparently you're all right, with Aretha and this apartment.

SYLVIA. (*going to the mantel, picking out the photo of her daughter*) And a few other goodies. Mainly my Lila.

LEATRICE. (*looking at the photograph*) No one ever understood how you had such a lovely, *normal* child.

SYLVIA. Me either. I lucked out, I just loved her. Do you know, I've made sixty-three films and she's by far my best production.

LEATRICE. (*crossing to bar*) Speaking of that, whatever happened to your last . . . ?

SYLVIA. Husband?

LEATRICE. Number eight.

SYLVIA. Seven.

LEATRICE. I always thought there was a number eight.

SYLVIA. Well, there was, but I had it annulled so it doesn't count. Even the church says it doesn't.
LEATRICE. I wouldn't think the church would have anything to say about you — period.
SYLVIA. I beg your pardon. I'm still a practicing Catholic. I go to mass every Sunday and I go to confession and communion.
LEATRICE. But with eight husbands . . .
SYLVIA. Seven!
LEATRICE. All right, seven. How do they even let you inside a church?
SYLVIA. (*sighing, perching on the* S.L. *arm-rest of sofa*) None of my husbands was Catholic. I was never married in a Catholic ceremony, so the church doesn't recognize them as marriages to begin with. (*crossing herself, ending up with her arms raised above her head, hands clasped dramatically*) In nomine patris et fille et spiritus sancti. Amen!
LEATRICE. (*sitting with her drink in chair* S.R. *of sofa*) I played three nuns and I never knew that.

(*ARETHA comes in with another platter, goes to SYLVIA.*)

SYLVIA. And I'm a Catholic and I never played a nun. Now, isn't that amazing?
ARETHA. No. The church may do some dumb things, but they draw the line at letting you play a nun.
SYLVIA. (*as LEATRICE chokes back a laugh*) Aretha, why don't you be an angel and —
ARETHA. Oh! Bad news from the kitchen. The boll weevils done got the whole cotton crop!
SYLVIA. Well, then — why don't you plant a *new* crop? I'll have the sprayers in on Monday.

ARETHA. Yes'um. (*curtsies, then starts for the kitchen, singing a long:*) "Ohhhhhhh . . . (*Halfway there, she breaks into song.*) — Nobody knows the trouble I've seen." (*exits*)

LEATRICE. Sylvia, the way you talk to her!

SYLVIA. Oh, Aretha understands, we just kid around. I mean — after five years.

LEATRICE. Five years!

SYLVIA. Why do you say it like that?

LEATRICE. Well, uh — that's a long run for you, isn't it?

SYLVIA. We're talking about help, not husbands.

LEATRICE. Well, speaking of husbands, would you be so kind as to tell me why you took mine?

SYLVIA. Don't be ridiculous — I took him *because* he was yours.

LEATRICE. (*laughing*) Well, you certainly got what you were looking for, didn't you?

SYLVIA. (*laughing also*) I sure did. That was one that backfired. (*cupping hands, calling out*) Tilt!

LEATRICE. (*laughing*) I can't tell you how many nights I giggled myself to sleep into my pillow over that.

SYLVIA. What an adorable mental picture that paints. (*as LEATRICE continues to laugh*) I'm glad someone had some fun out of it. So handsome on the outside . . .

LEATRICE. So witty.

SYLVIA. So bright.

LEATRICE. So debonair.

SYLVIA. — And the worst case of premature ejaculation in recorded history!

LEATRICE & SYLVIA. He said I got him too excited!

SYLVIA. You, too? Now, you see, if we'd been friends, we could have spared each other that!

LEATRICE. Wait a minute, there's something not quite right there. If we'd been friends, *I* could have spared *you* that. What would you have done for me?

SYLVIA. Well . . . I could have told you that Sydney Kroll intended for *Taj Mahal* to be the biggest disaster in film history because his backers needed a huge tax write-off.

LEATRICE. You knew that before they made it?

SYLVIA. (*nodding*) Why do you think I turned it down?

LEATRICE. I didn't know they ever offered it to you.

SYLVIA. They did. But I suggested *you*.

LEATRICE. You got me into that! Why, you —

SYLVIA. Ah-ah, you laughed at my honeymoon. Fair's fair.

LEATRICE. There's something not right there either. *Taj Mahal* was way before we ever started feuding.

SYLVIA. Well, it may have been before *we* ever started feuding. But *I* had started without you!

LEATRICE. Why, I'd never done anything to you.

SYLVIA. Oh, everybody was always going around saying what a bitch I was . . .

LEATRICE. Well, you were.

SYLVIA. I was candid, I said what was on my mind. I fought for what I believed in.

LEATRICE. (*standing*) Well, what was I doing? Conspiring with the Japanese to bomb Pearl Harbor!

SYLVIA. (*also standing*) No, but everyone was forever chirping about what an angel you were. Always spreading joy, joy, joy! Oh, so sweet, so adorable, so marvelous to work with, so generous, so giving, so —

LEATRICE. — so what? *Taj Mahal* almost ended my career.

SYLVIA. Your career ended because too many diabetics were advised not to see your pictures.

LEATRICE. And your career ended when audiences wanted to see more than just—(*brushing a finger across SYLVIA's cheek, then examining her finger*)—make-up!

SYLVIA. Your last picture was supposed to be a love story, but they had to release it as science fiction.

LEATRICE. Your last picture's still hanging in the post office.

SYLVIA. You made your *first* picture before they *had* post offices.

LEATRICE. Tell me, sweetheart, what was Hollywood like before sound came in?

SYLVIA. Just like it was when you arrived in a covered wagon, dear.

LEATRICE. At least I was sitting in it—not pulling it.

SYLVIA. Are you calling me a cow?

LEATRICE. You guessed! You want to talk more livestock, let's talk about your husbands! (*ARETHA enters with more canapes.*)

SYLVIA. At least I married everyone I—

LEATRICE. Watch it, dear!

SYLVIA. (*going after her*) Watch this, you little—

ARETHA. Ladies, ladies!

SYLVIA. We were just having a heart-to-heart.

ARETHA. I'm not going to be responsible for any breakage. Mrs. Coulter—(*The doorbell rings; ARETHA, LEATRICE and SYLVIA freeze.*)

LEATRICE. Mr. Klemmer!

ARETHA. They didn't buzz from downstairs, they usually—

SYLVIA. Holy Mother of God—now what'll we do?

LEATRICE. Well, I'm going to sit right here and pretend that none of this is happening.

SYLVIA. Look, let's just see what he says. How much he offers.

LEATRICE. (*sitting in chair, far* S.R.) Better be a fortune. Plus California, Oregon and General Motors. (*To appear nonchalant, she takes a magazine from the rack next to the chair, looks at the cover, starts to thumb through it, then flips back to the cover, stares at it and smiles.*)

SYLVIA. (*also sitting in chair next to her*) Now, Leatrice. (*The doorbell rings again, LEATRICE puts the magazine next to her side, away from SYLVIA.*) Aretha! (*ARETHA heads for the door.*)

ARETHA. Coming . . .

SYLVIA. Let's just play it like we don't really care.

LEATRICE. (*indicating herself*) Well, *we* don't! (*Sound of door opening is heard.*)

MAN'S VOICE. Aretha?

ARETHA. Yes, but . . .

MAN'S VOICE. Our little Aretha who's leaving us?

ARETHA. (*now alarmed*) No, not that one!

(*A slim, young, perky, good-looking black man, BOOM-BOOM JOHNSON, immaculately dressed in dinner clothes [tails] enters carrying a portable cassette recorder and places it on the piano. ARETHA follows him as SYLVIA and LEATRICE stare in confused wonder. LEATRICE slips the magazine behind her back.*)

BOOM-BOOM. Oh, now, how many Arethas can there be?

ARETHA. I'm afraid you have the wrong one!

BOOM-BOOM. Now, there's nothing to be afraid of. I'm your surprise guest from Chippendale's Supper Club.

ARETHA. Wait a minute. Didn't you get the message?
BOOM-BOOM. Not another word. (*hands her an envelope*) Here's your very own copy of the following telegram. Come, sit. (*He sits her in the third* S.R. *chair, closest to* C.S. *He glances around, is somewhat perplexed to find his audience consists of only two rather elegant white ladies, bows to them and then faces ARETHA to sing a little a cappella verse.*)
Happy wedding to you
Aretha, our dear
Your guy is so neat
Your guy is so sweet
Within a year
We wanna hear
The pitter patter
Of little feet!
Love, the gang.

P.S. But for *now*—we've sent you *this little treat!*

(*He reaches behind him, presses the "play" button on the recorder. [Aretha Franklin's recording of "Respect" blasts forth.] Note: or any other appropriate song with a good strong "stripping beat."*
The strip as done in the original company included the following bits of business: his dinner clothes are completely breakaway, designed with velcro. He wore top hat, tails, white gloves and a white silk scarf around his neck. When these were stripped off, he wore a breakaway pair of French shorts, under that a smaller breakaway pair of bikini shorts and under that a gold-tassled G-string or posing strap. On his behind, a gold-spangled halfmoon decorated one cheek and a gold-spangled star was glued on the other.

He started out the dance by merely doing some subtle hip gyrations, then he crossed behind SYLVIA, taking his gloves off seductively and dropping them in her lap. He then moved around behind LEATRICE, taking his silk scarf off and daintily draping it around her neck. He then moved C.S. for some real bumping and grinding, reaching behind him and pulling off the tails which were detachable and slapping them down on the chair, S.L. He removed the rest of his coat and dropped it on the sofa. He then moved to ARETHA, took his top hat off and jammed it down on her head. Then, he moved around and came in between SYLVIA and LEATRICE, slipping off the halves of his red suspenders and handing one half to each of the astonished ladies. They held on as he bumped and grinded, finally pulling off his breakaway dinner shirt. The only thing remaining above his waist was his bow tie. After this, he did some fancy steps moving to S.L. Then, he did a running somersault toward ARETHA and pulled her into the action. While doing this, he unloosened his pants so they would fall down to his ankles as he started to dance with her. When he finally pulled the pants off completely, ARETHA, trying to escape, fell to the floor and he straddled her and danced over her body. He moved to LEATRICE, took her by the hand and stood her up and bumped her hips with his. He then took SYLVIA by the hand and she, by this time, was so lost in the music, she began gyrating with him, doing the frug, the twist, etc. He quickly went to ARETHA, who was crawling on her hands and knees, S.L., to get away and rode her as one would ride a pony. She finally managed to get up and run behind the sofa. At this point, he yanked off the brea-

kaway shorts, sat down on the coffee table, bumped his behind as he traveled the length of it, all the while smiling broadly at the two ladies. He then jumped up onto the coffee table, did a few more bumps and grinds and ripped off the bikini briefs to reveal the spangled posing strap. He went once more to give LEATRICE's behind a final bump, once more to SYLVIA, and a final hip bump to ARETHA, who did a split on the final beat of the number. [Note: If the actress can't do a split, he can give her a hip bump, knocking her into the chair, S.L.]

After the strip, the two ladies stand in silence as ARETHA goes from spot to spot, picking up each article of clothing and gathering them to her. She keeps hidden in one hand the pair of bikini briefs. When she finally hands the pile to the stripper, she goes to wipe her forehead with the hand that holds the briefs; she is surprised by this and hands them gingerly to BOOM-BOOM.)

ARETHA. It is a little bit nippy out. Maybe you'd like to—reconstitute yourself in the . . . bedroom over there. I'm sure Mrs.—Glenn wouldn't mind, would you?

SYLVIA. Not at all, Not at all. (*crossing to BOOM-BOOM*) Perhaps I can be of some assistance! (*BOOM-BOOM exits into the bedroom.*)

LEATRICE. Sylvia!

SYLVIA. Oh, damn! (*All the ladies sit* S.R. *ARETHA looks at LEATRICE who is trying desperately not to laugh.*)

ARETHA. (*after a long silence, during which the ladies*

have simply been sitting there looking front) Well . . . that was *something*, wasn't it?

LEATRICE. Do you have performances every night or only during full moon?

ARETHA. Miss Glenn, you shouldn't have gone to all that bother. But—it was fun, wasn't it?

SYLVIA. Yes. He was supposed to come later. Much later, but—what the hay!

ARETHA. (*making her escape*) I'll just check in the kitchen, I think I left some canapes in the oven.

SYLVIA. We didn't tell you Aretha's getting married — again, did we?

LEATRICE. No, Sylvia, you haven't told me a lot of things. (*standing, with the magazine rolled up in her hand*) You must think I'm deaf, dumb and blind!

SYLVIA. Why, Leatrice—

LEATRICE. Sylvia, I like the play. And in the past I've admired some of your acting, some of your persona has been entertaining at times. But I do not like—your tricks, your games, your—

SYLVIA. Now, wait a minute. That was a long time ago. That was in Hollywood. We're both older and wiser now. And we're talking about the theater, the legitimate theater where there's no room for—

LEATRICE. I'm talking about honesty and truthfulness and laying the cards on the table.

SYLVIA. Well, then you're talking to the right gal. If I'm anything I'm a straight shooter.

LEATRICE. Raise your right hand and swear to God.

SYLVIA. (*raising her hand, looking up*) I swear to God! (*dropping her hand, heading toward the bar*) There, that's all settled. Now, let's drink to—

LEATRICE. (*picking up photo from behind sofa*)— Imelda Marcos!

SYLVIA. Imelda Marcos? The Barefoot Contessa. Imelda Marcos indeed!

LEATRICE. (*handing the picture to her*) Funny, she always spoke well of you. *Dorothy!*)

SYLVIA. Oh, shit!

LEATRICE. (*unrolling the magazine, then reading*) "Mrs. Dorothy Coulter, 758 Park Ave., Apt. 8D, New York City, New York, 10021." And did you know that Aretha has been with you for three years instead of five. You must have lost a couple of years. Boozing, no doubt.

SYLVIA. It was all a little white lie. I told it mostly so Mr. Klemmer'd think — Leatrice, this play is so right for the two of us.

LEATRICE. The play is perfect for two actresses of "a certain age." But you are not one of them. Or if you are — I am not. Mr. Klemmer can have you with my heartfelt sympathies. And he can have someone else as well.

SYLVIA. Everyone else is either dead or we're not speaking.

LEATRICE. I'm going to be late for "21." (*calling out*) Aretha, my cape please!

SYLVIA. Oh, Leatrice, can't we talk about this like two sensible adults?

LEATRICE. We're not two sensible adults. We're one sensible adult and one sad, pitiful —

SYLVIA. All right, so I'm not sitting on a stack of blue chips as high as —

LEATRICE. Spare me the details — please! Nothing has changed. You're still the same scheming, mischievous, lying, sordid little tramp you always were.

SYLVIA. What do you mean — sordid! (*As ARETHA enters with her cape, LEATRICE crosses to retrieve it.*)

LEATRICE. Thank you, Aretha. Do give my best to

Mrs. Coulter—(*passing SYLVIA on her way to the foyer*) *and* Imelda Marcos.

SYLVIA. Your compassion and generosity are truly touching. I hope you choke to death at "21."

LEATRICE. Thank you. (*about to leave*)

SYLVIA. (*calling after her*) By the way, *I* was the one that started the fire in your dressing room trailer!

LEATRICE. (*turning back*) Oh, that's all right. It was my secretary who put Ex-Lax in your coffee every morning. (*pats SYLVIA on the cheek and quickly leaves*)

SYLVIA. (*screaming after her*) Well, I was the one who had that snake put in your make-up kit so you'd die of hysterics when—(*The front door slams.*)

ARETHA. Um-umm! And I thought I was heavy when I was into my voodoo period.

SYLVIA. I could tell her a few other things I arranged.

ARETHA. We should have rehearsed more. Except I think we had her fooled up until the appearance of Mr. Gypsy Rose Leroy.

SYLVIA. (*walking DS., starting to kick the back of the sofa*) Goddam her and her haughty self-righteous—(*discovering LEATRICE's purse on the table backing the sofa*)—What do we have here? So busy playing her big exit scene, she forgot her purse! I ought to hide it from her, deny it was ever here, take all her credit cards and clean out Bloomingdale's and Saks. (*sits in chair near sofa, dumps the contents of the purse into her lap, notices a yellow piece of paper*) Hmn . . . this yellow paper looks familiar. (*opening it, starting to read*) "Dear Miss Monsée. We're sorry to report that your request for an additional thirteen weeks of *unemployment* insurance has been turned down due to insufficient earnings in the last fiscal year. However, a monthly allotment of two hundred and thirty dollars in *food stamps* will be provided you. On top of this, your union, Screen Actors Guild, gives you a — (*The doorbell rings. SYLVIA, pure delight spread over her face, turns to ARETHA as she puts the purse and letter behind her back and speaks in a delighted growl.*) Aretha — let Leatrice back in.

ARETHA. (*on her way to the door*) Oh, my God . . .

SYLVIA. Him, too — but only if he says "May I?"

LEATRICE. (*She hurries in, heading for the chair, DS.R.*) I was in such a hurry to get out of here, I forgot my bag. And now I'm going to be late for "21." (*looking behind the cushion*)

SYLVIA. (*holding the purse and unemployment letter in front of her, speaking once more in baby talk*) — Yes, hers gonna be late for "21." Ittsy poo. Itsa bad liddle Leatrice! (*then in her own voice*) And do you know how stupid I am? All these years of going to "21" and I never knew they accepted food stamps.

LEATRICE. (*gasping*) Why, you cheap, lying, snooping —

SYLVIA. Hypocrite, is that the word you're looking for?

LEATRICE. Cheap, lying, snooping . . .

SYLVIA. Oh, go ahead, say it. You want to say the "C" word, don't you? *don't you?*

LEATRICE. The "C" word??? Try the whole bloody alphabet!

SYLVIA. (*waving the letter in front of LEATRICE's nose*) I'm going to sell this to Liz Smith. (*LEATRICE begins to chase SYLVIA, who turns and runs S.L., up between the mantel and sofa, then eventually over to the piano.*)

LEATRICE. Ahh! You wouldn't dare!

SYLVIA. Miss Haughty High Horse is obviously flat-ass, down at the heels bloody broke.

LEATRICE. I may be broke but I'm not mentally ill! (*By this time, they're both by the piano, SYLVIA hikes her dress up a bit, ready for battle.*)

SYLVIA. You will be when I get through with you!

LEATRICE. I despise you—you and all of your damned autographed, badly-framed photographs! (*LEATRICE grabs hold of the shawl-throw on the piano, upon which the pictures stand, gives it a furious yank that sends them all crashing. She then strides* DS.C. *SYLVIA follows her in a screaming rage.*)

SYLVIA. No, not my pictures! You damn woman!

ARETHA. Wait! Wait, what if Mr. Klemmer shows up!

SYLVIA & LEATRICE. Screw Mr. Klemmer! (*SYLVIA, goes to kick LEATRICE. As she does, LEATRICE snatches SYLVIA's wig, turns and runs, shrieking in delight. SYLVIA runs after her and pulls LEATRICE's wig off from behind. LEATRICE lets out a yelp, turns and the ladies come together* DS.C., *swatting each other, using their wigs as weapons.*)

CURTAIN

ACT TWO

Scene 1

The 42nd Street I.R.T. station. A bank of three pay phones face the house. A graffitied brick wall backs the phones. A wire trash basket containing papers, odds and ends, a broken umbrella, sits to the side. The unseen subway tracks run alongside the orchestra pit.

A harried MARTIN KLEMMER, wearing an overcoat, is waiting for a train, having missed one, which we just hear pulling away as the lights come up on this scene. He glances at the phones, rifles through his pockets — he has no change. He quickly goes to each phone, beginning with the s.r. *one, and checks their coin returns for change. Empty. He pushes "0" for the operator on the number 1,* s.l. *phone.*

MARTIN. Excuse me, operator, but I've just put my seventh quarter in this phone and I still can't get a dial tone . . . Of course, I'm sure. Who do you think you're talking to? This is Martin Klemmer, producer of the Off-Broadway hit, *Craps* . . . Oh, I see. All right, Miss, may I please have your full name, social security number, and may I please speak to your supervisor. I am sick and tired of the phone company and I — . . . Oh, you will? . . . Ah, thank you . . . thank you, Brenda. (*He hangs up, we hear money falling into the coin return.*) Jackpot! (*scoops up the money, goes to the middle phone, #2, and punches in a number*) Hello, Marks Wholesale Unisex Fashion Outlet? . . . May I please speak to Mr. Sidney Marks? . . . He's on long distance, how long? . . . Would you have him get right back to Martin Klemmer. I'm at . . . Sardi's restaurant! (*looks at this phone to get the number*) It's 987-6532 . . . Yes, Sardi's, goodbye. (*hangs up, goes to phone #3, S.R. phone, puts a quarter in and punches in a number*) Denise, how many times do I have to tell you—always answer the phone with "The Off-Broadway hit, *Craps*. May I help you, please?" It's so uncouth when you only say *"Craps!"* . . . (*suddenly bellows*) What? That sleazy scuzz-head is drunk again! Well, you find his understudy and get right back to me at . . . (*glances at 3rd phone*) . . . 949-0663. (*The 2nd phone rings.*) Yeah, Just find him. (*hangs up, snatches up 2nd phone, speaks in a thick French accent*) Bon soir, Sardi's. May I help you, please? . . . Who? . . . Mr. Klemmer? Why of course. One moment, please. (*calling out*) Suzette, page our Mr. Klemmer. He'll be right with you, sir. (*A loud fire engine siren echoes down through the subway and is quickly gone. KLEMMER looks up, thinks fast as he calls out:*) Phillipe, not so much flambé on ze crepes! (*then*) Your telephone, sir. (*as himself*) Thank you, Andre, and keep the change . . . (*then*) Okay, Sidney, I'm sitting here with Leatrice and Sylvia right now so what's the deal? Yeah . . . yeah . . . yeah . . . They love it so much, they want to go into rehearsal yesterday! . . . Look, Sidney, I'm telling you, this is pure gold, but I can't string them along. These are big stars! . . . Okay, I'll be honest with you, I've got three other money guys lined up with their tongues hanging out . . . No, it's not a pretty picture. Sidney, if you hesitate even for a minute—(*He checks the subway tracks.*)—you're gonna miss the train. So what's the deal, yes or no . . . on or off? (*The 3rd phone rings.*) . . . Hold on, Sidney . . . you just bought yourself another minute. (*grabs phone #3 as he covers the mouthpiece of #2*) Denise, what's up? . . . Whaddaya mean, the understudy's drunk, too! . . . They got drunk together? How'd that happen? I thought they were supposed to take turns. (*returns to phone #2, holds #3 against his side*) Listen, Sydney, Leatrice and Sylvia are such cut-ups. And they cannot wait to meet you. And guess what? (*Phone #1 rings. He looks from #3 to #2 to it, confused.*) Sydney, hold on, we're having a fire drill. (*puts the other receivers on the ledge and picks up #1*) Hello? . . . No . . . no, this is not the Suicide Hotline, joker. So, what do you say to that? . . . No, don't do that! . . . Turn off the oven . . . don't light a match, open a window. Take a deep breath . . . No, not in the oven, by the window! Look, take a deep breath and hold on! (*muttering to himself as he picks up phone #2*) And I thought the theater was tough. (*then*) And Sydney, guess what? Sylvia and Leatrice have even agreed to come to your son's bar mitzvah next month . . . Yes. Well, think about that for a minute and a half. (*puts receiver down, returns to phone #3*) Denise, you've gotta sober 'em up . . . No, not both, just one of them! . . . Completely out? . . . What? *Me* go on? I haven't acted in years. (*Holding the receiver to his chest, he strikes a dramatic pose, then speaks to Denise.*) Hold on. (*As he passes phone #2, he picks it up quickly and laughing, says*:) What a script! (*to phone #1*) How we doin', pal? . . . What? . . . I can't understand a word you're saying . . . Of course, I want you to *exhale*! . . . What do you mean you've got nothing to live for? Of course, you've got something to live for. Have you ever seen the Off-Broadway hit, *Craps*? . . . Well, you're gonna see it tonight. I'm going to give you two free tick—two half-price tickets . . . Yes, hold on, I'll give you the details. (*back to phone #2*) Okay, Sydney, what is it? Do I get the money, yes or no? . . . What? . . . Your wife, Esther, wants to say hello to who? . . . Well, Sydney, this is a big star, I just can't drag Sylvia Glenn across a restaurant to— . . . is that a firm promise? . . . Okay, but that's a deal! (*calling out*) Andre? Escort Miss Glenn to the phone, please. (*as Andre*) Oui, Monsieur. (*back to Sydney*) Get Esther. She's on her way. (*back to 3rd phone*) Okay, Denise, this is it—I need somebody, anybody, to go on for tonight and oh, I need two half-price tickets for tonight under the name of—(*back to 1st phone*)— What's your name, pal? . . . Norbert Klug! . . . Terrific! (*back to 3rd phone*) Norbert Klug . . . Denise, stop laughing. (*back to 1st phone*) Hey, Norbie. I've got those tickets for you tonight, they'll be at the box office under your name and— . . . You've got no one to go with? . . . No, wait a minute, when you get to the theater, there will be a girl at the door. Her name's Denise. Yeah, she's dying to— . . . crazy to meet you . . . Well, no, she's not tall and blonde . . . Well, she's got a slight hair problem . . . Look, she'll be wearing a hat! (*puts 1st and 3rd phone receivers together*) Norbert, Denise. Denise, meet Norbie. Have a wonderful life, see you in paradise, you two lovebirds. (*He hangs up the 1st and 3rd phones. He takes a deep breath, strikes a pose, throws back his head and speaks in a striking imitation of SYLVIA GLENN's telephone voice.*) Hello, Esther . . . Yes, this is Sylvia Glenn . . . ! (*Then her laugh "Ah-ha-ha-ha!" as the loud sound of a subway train approaches and KLEMMER looks anxiously down the tracks.*) You'll have to speak up, Esther. Here comes the dessert cart!

BLACKOUT

LEGENDS

Scene 2

The apartment is a mess. Both combatants, now tempersome as wet cats, are winded. LEATRICE, holding an ice bag to her head, sits in far S.R. chair. Both ladies' wigs are off, LEATRICE's is on the piano. SYLVIA sits in far S.L. chair; her wig rests atop the lamp behind that chair. SYLVIA is minus one shoe and her dress is ripped up one side.

A POLICEMAN, in his thirties, is finishing writing his report. ARETHA, a little the worse for wear, is slumped in a chair between the ladies. The coffee table is tipped on its side.

POLICEMAN. All right, ladies, I'll just put down here under ages . . . "indeterminate."

LEATRICE. Brilliant!

SYLVIA. Terrific!

POLICEMAN. Now, let me make sure that I have the story straight. This apartment that you trashed isn't yours and it isn't yours? I mean, neither one of you lives here.

LEATRICE. We were just rehearsing a play we might do.

SYLVIA. Yes, we were just visiting. It belongs to Dorothy Coulter, a very good friend of mine.

POLICEMAN. Well, by the looks of things, I guess I'd rather rehearse at a friend's house too. (*He rights the tipped-over coffee table.*)

LEATRICE. Aretha, would you be a dear and please pass me my wig?

SYLVIA. (*standing*) Please pass the wig. What is that color, Greer Garson pink?

ARETHA. Ladies, ladies.

SYLVIA. (*turning, spots her wig atop the lamp,* S.L.) Oh — there you are! (*picking it up and putting it on her head*) Aretha, would you be a dear and help me reconstitute myself?

LEATRICE. (*stands and takes her wig from ARETHA, sets it atop her head*) And about time. Very few women can wear aluminum foil. (*turns, facing* US., *bumps her hip toward SYLVIA, then walks to the mirror on the piano and straightens her wig out*)

SYLVIA. (*opening the bedroom door*) Oh, you really are —

BOOM-BOOM. (*offstage; loud*) Is it safe to come out now?

SYLVIA. Ah, Leatrice, I almost forgot — your friend.

LEATRICE. *My* friend!

(*SYLVIA enters the bedroom as BOOM-BOOM comes out; he and the POLICEMAN look each other over.*)

POLICEMAN. (*to BOOM-BOOM*) Did you have anything to do with this mess?

BOOM-BOOM. No, I was in the bedroom.

POLICEMAN. (*writing in his book now*) What's your name?

BOOM-BOOM. B.B. Johnson.

POLICEMAN. What's the B.B. stand for?

BOOM-BOOM. Boom-Boom.

POLICEMAN. Boom-Boom — where do you work?

BOOM-BOOM. Chippendale's.

POLICEMAN. How do you spell it?

BOOM-BOOM. Like the furniture.

POLICEMAN. What do you do?

BOOM-BOOM. Stripper.

POLICEMAN. Got it. Strips paint off furniture. So what were you doing here — a job?

BOOM-BOOM. Yes.
POLICEMAN. In the bedroom?
BOOM-BOOM. No, I was putting my clothes on in the bedroom.
POLICEMAN. Oh, getting out of your work clothes?
BOOM-BOOM. No, getting *into* my work clothes.
POLICEMAN. Fancy organization you work for.
BOOM-BOOM. Satisfaction guaranteed.
POLICEMAN. You know, my wife's having some trouble in our bedroom. Maybe you could come over and —
BOOM-BOOM. (*handing him a card*) My card. Have your wife call me.
POLICEMAN. I really appreciate that. She's got this great old chest, but it's a mess.
BOOM-BOOM. I'd be happy to take a look at it.
POLICEMAN. Thank you very much.
BOOM-BOOM. You're welcome.
POLICEMAN. Goodbye.
BOOM-BOOM. (*to LEATRICE*) Goodnight, Miss.
LEATRICE. Goodnight. (*He leaves.*)
POLICEMAN. Is he really that good?
LEATRICE. You'll have to ask your wife.

(*SYLVIA and ARETHA, lugging a vacuum cleaner, come out of the bedroom. The POLICEMAN looks from SYLVIA to LEATRICE, who has come DS. to sit on the sofa.*)

POLICEMAN. Say, wait a minute. I didn't recognize you at first without your hair, but — now I know who you are. The two of you! You're Leatrice Monsen —
LEATRICE. Mon-sée.
POLICEMAN. And you're Sylvia —
SYLVIA. (*sitting, chair* S.L.) Glenn!

POLICEMAN. Sure, sure! I've seen you both a lot on "The Late, Late Show." Say, do you get paid every time they show your movies?

LEATRICE. (*wailing*) No!

SYLVIA. Now they do, but not when we made 'em, goddam-it-to-hell and Louis B. Mayer!

POLICEMAN. That's too bad. I wonder—you wouldn't mind giving me your autograph, would you?

LEATRICE. Why no, not at all.

POLICEMAN. (*as LEATRICE signs*) My mother used to see all your movies when she was a little girl.

SYLVIA. (*cackling*) So did I.

POLICEMAN. (*crossing to SYLVIA with his pad*) And you, Miss Glenn?

SYLVIA. Of course, to whom?

POLICEMAN. To Julia. She's my grandmother. She was always crazy about you.

LEATRICE. (*cackling*) So was mine.

SYLVIA. There. Then I take it we're even and there won't be any more—

POLICEMAN. Oh, no, no. I hope you didn't misunderstand. I still have to file my report.

LEATRICE. You mean after all that mother and grandmother bit?

POLICEMAN. I'm one of the new breed, we're uncorruptible.

LEATRICE. I hope you end up in one of those tiny little cubicles smack in the center of Lincoln Tunnel!

SYLVIA. At rush hour. With exhaust fumes as deadly as nerve gas.

LEATRICE. And when your next child is born and people ask if it's a boy or a girl—I hope you have to hesitate an hour before answering.

POLICEMAN. Then I take it autographed pictures are out.

SYLVIA & LEATRICE. Oh, get out! (*The phone rings.*)
POLICEMAN. (*exiting*) Right. Goodnight, ladies.
SYLVIA. I bought fifty tickets to the Policemen's Ball one year! It'll be a merry day in . . . (*She picks up the receiver; her phone voice.*)Hello . . . Yes, this is Sylvia Glenn . . . I beg your pardon, a party? (*then*) Oh, honestly, Doris, this is no time to kid around about parties . . . Who? . . . Sean Penn is coming with Madonna? I don't care if Billy Graham is coming with Boy George! (*slams the phone down*)
LEATRICE. You'd be a joy to work with, you really would.
SYLVIA. Well, that's something we don't have to worry about, isn't it?
LEATRICE. I don't know why, but I'm hungry.
SYLVIA. Well, why don't you call up "21" and have them send something over? Aretha will take the food stamps down to the taxi when it arrives.
ARETHA. Physical exercise always works up a good, healthy—(*SYLVIA, suddenly glassy-eyed and wobbly, falls back onto the sofa, a hand to her head.*)
SYLVIA. Oh . . . Aretha, help me! . . . Help!
LEATRICE. Sylvia! What's the matter.
ARETHA. Oh, my Lord!
SYLVIA. Coca-Cola . . . Pepsi . . .
ARETHA. Oh . . . Okay . . . a little Coca-Cola coming right up! (*splashes a little cola in a glass at the bar*)
LEATRICE. What is it?
SYLVIA. I forgot to eat . . . I skipped a meal . . .
ARETHA. Here you go . . . You just need a little bit, you'll be all right. (*handing it to her*)
LEATRICE. Aretha, what is it?
ARETHA. Miss Glenn's diabetic. She takes care of it, but now she needs a little sugar fix, huh, baby? What else

can I get you?

SYLVIA. Prunes . . . apricots . . . anything like that.

ARETHA. Okay . . . won't be a moment. (*to LEATRICE*) Pour her a little more cola. (*runs out into the kitchen*)

LEATRICE. (*taking her glass, crossing to the bar*) Shouldn't we call a doctor?

SYLVIA. I just gotta get my blood sugar up. Need something sweet.

LEATRICE. Something sweet? Oh, there's some cookies over here. (*picking up a plate from the* S.R. *table*)

SYLVIA. Cookies?

LEATRICE. (*pulling the cellophane back*) Yes. They look wonderful. No, they're brownies.

SYLVIA. Oh, fine. (*LEATRICE hurries to SYLVIA, who takes a brownie and begins munching on it.*) Ummm, good, fudge.

LEATRICE. Well, I don't mind if I do. Ummm, ummm, they are good. (*They both chew in silence for a while.*) Diabetes, I didn't know you had diabetes.

SYLVIA. Neither did I, til a couple of years ago. Then suddenly, whammo — another one of life's surprises!

LEATRICE. I know. I've had a few of those myself. (*then sweetly*) Oh, Sylvia, I'm so sorry. I really am. I hope it's not painful or anything like that.

SYLVIA. Oh, listen to that. You should have played Melanie in *Gone With The Wind*. You would have made Olivia de Havilland **look** like Captain Bligh.

LEATRICE. I **was being** sincere!

SYLVIA. Oh, come now. (*mimicking her*) Oh, Sylvia, I'm so sorry. I hope it's not anything painful —

LEATRICE. (*standing*) Oh, stop it, stop it! Can't you ever take anything at face value? Do you always make fun of everyone? (*quickly gathering her things*) I don't have time for any of this . . .

SYLVIA. Oh, Leatrice . . .

LEATRICE. You just won't give up, will you? Aren't you tired of yourself by now?

SYLVIA. Yes!

LEATRICE. Good! That makes millions of us! And when Mr. Klemmer comes, you can tell him to dig up someone else! (*on her way out*)

SYLVIA. (standing) If you're that broke then why would you turn down a play with Paul Newman?

LEATRICE. I am not turning down Paul Newman. I am turning you down. Life is far too short. (*LEATRICE starts out.*)

SYLVIA. (*She crosses after her and shouts.*) Don't you ever get frightened?

LEATRICE. (*stops in foyer*) Yes!

SYLVIA. And don't you ever get just plain lonely.

LEATRICE. Yes!

(*ARETHA enters with a bowl of fruit.*)

SYLVIA. Well, then why don't you do the play, for God's sake!

ARETHA. Are you two mixing it up again? What is the matter with you?

SYLVIA. The woman's crazy!

LEATRICE. (*stepping down to sofa*) I'm off for good this time, Aretha.

ARETHA. Now, now, Miss Monsée. (*She spots the plate of brownies.*) Oh, my Lord, Where did you ever find these? (*picks the plate up*)

LEATRICE. Her blood sugar is back up. I'm going.

ARETHA. (*crossing to the phone*) You're not going

anywhere yet, Miss Monsée. Just hold on, hold on a minute. (*She dials.*) Hello . . . Ella Mae Sue Ella, honey? . . . Those fudge brownies that you brought over, were those just double fudge brownies or were they— . . . Oh, my God! . . . Well, someone got a hold of one of them and ate it.

LEATRICE. I had one too. It was yummy.

ARETHA. Yummy! Ummm! (*into phone*) Two people got a hold of two of 'em and ate 'em. Look, I've got an emergency here. I'll talk to you tomorrow . . . What? . . . All right . . . 'bye. (*hangs up*)

SYLVIA. Now, what was all that about?

LEATRICE. We haven't been poisoned?

ARETHA. Ella Mae Sue Ella says to wish you all a happy trip!

LEATRICE. I'm not going on any trip with her!

ARETHA. (*guiding LEATRICE*) Miss Monsée, take off your cape and sit down. Now, come along and do as I say. Now, don't panic, ladies, but you have each ingested one of Ella Mae Sue Ella's Black Magic Voodoo-Whoodoo Juju Brownies. What I'm trying to say is: those brownies are made with—hashish. (*sits her S.L. end of sofa*)

LEATRICE. Hashish!

SYLVIA. Dope? You mean—dope!

ARETHA. If you want to call it that, yes. It's hashish!

LEATRICE. Oh, dear, oh, dear—whatever will we do?

SYLVIA. (*pirouetting, flapping her arms a la* Swan Lake) Oh, you—you'll probably turn into a swan and do a pas de quatre all by yourself.

ARETHA. Ah-ah, this is no time for fussin'. This is a time for serious thought. Now you two listen to me. I may not know much about being a movie star, but I do know about Ella Mae Sue Ella's Black Magic Voodoo Whoodoo Juju Brownies.

LEATRICE. Well, what happens, will we get crazy?

SYLVIA. (*silly question*) Now, Leatrice . . .

LEATRICE. I mean, will we get *crazier*.

ARETHA. How many animals in a zoo? Hash brownies affect different people different ways. Some people sort of — wham, like a velvet hammer — out for the count. And some fly right on up to the ceiling. Some hallucinate just a little. And some folks get extremely chatty. Like they had truth serum, it all hangs out.

LEATRICE. Oh, dear . . .

ARETHA. (*flopping on the sofa*) And some just sit and think. Others just laugh, happy as piss clams at high tide.

SYLVIA. Well, how long before this begins, what are the signs?

ARETHA. It depends on your system. A couple of minutes. Five, ten, fifteen. 'Round there.

LEATRICE. (*standing*) I don't feel a thing. I'm going home!

ARETHA. That's the first sign! Miss Monsée, you do not want to be out there in the world when this thing hits you. You better keep your tail in here.

LEATRICE. We won't begin to fight again?

ARETHA. No, no. It hardly ever makes people feisty. In fact, it makes most people mellow. But, of course, you two, the cobra and the mongoose.

SYLVIA. Jumpin' Saint Jude, but when Mr. Klemmer comes . . . ?

ARETHA. He better come soon. You all ain't got long before blast-off.

LEATRICE. Well, I still think I should go home!

ARETHA. Miss Monsée, think of yourself as a walking time bomb. Now you stay here with your friends.

LEATRICE. Friends!

ARETHA. (*stands*) Well, I'm your friend and so is Miss Glenn. Aren't you?

SYLVIA. I am — if she agrees to do the play.

LEATRICE. You see. That's just what I mean.

ARETHA. Now, ladies. Remember that picture with Miss Bankhead? *Lifeboat*? You two are in a lifeboat together and you don't want to rock it too much 'cause — ain't no tellin' who might fall out.

SYLVIA. All right now, what do we do?

ARETHA. I'll tell you what to do. You want to stuff your tummies with food. The fuller your stomach the less the hashish works. And you want to stay busy, active, don't just sit around. Now I'll get to work in the kitchen and you two — tidy up this place just in case he does show.

SYLVIA. Well, I don't feel a thing.

ARETHA. Oh, you'll be fine, girlfriend. The vacuum cleaner is here. The broom and dustpan are right around the corner there. Now I'll go hustle up some food and if you two start getting goofy, give a yell. Now take care and mind yourselves. (*ARETHA leaves. SYLVIA steps into the foyer to get a small broom and dustpan with a handle.*)

LEATRICE. Well, if Aretha's cooking for us — the least we can do is tidy up for her.

SYLVIA. (*returning with broom and dustpan*) You're right. (LEATRICE walks to the S.R. *lamp which is badly mangled.*)

LEATRICE. Oh, what a mess. Just look at this lamp! It looks like it's ready for Forest Lawn.

SYLVIA. (*picking up a broken photo*) Ahhhh — You smashed my Lana Turner.

LEATRICE. Didn't you always want to?

SYLVIA. Yes!

LEATRICE. Now, you sweep up and I'll vacuum. I just love to vacuum, sometimes when I'm blue I just vacuum and vacuum and it just does something for me. (*She sweeps up a mess* C.S. *without turning the machine on.*) Why did you ask if I ever got lonely?

SYLVIA. Oh, because I do. I get lonely, that's what I hate the most, I do believe — loneliness.

LEATRICE. You never give that impression at all. You always act as if you're not only giving the party, you're all the guests as well.

SYLVIA. Not true. That's just whistling past the graveyard. And speaking of which, that's what I hate about dying.

LEATRICE. What?

SYLVIA. Well, everyone's always sounding off about how we have to die alone. "You come into the world alone, you leave the world alone." I always thought it would be kind of nice if we all held hands and jumped together!

LEATRICE. But we'll be going in opposite directions.

SYLVIA. Aren't you afraid of dying?

LEATRICE. I'm not so much afraid of dying anymore, I mean leaving my body. I just hate to leave it in such a *mess*.

SYLVIA. Well, speaking of messes, we'd better step on it before the boss gets back. (*She steps on the vacuum button.*)

LEATRICE. (*Hearing the sound, amazed at the noise and suction, she holds the brush part up to her face.*) Oh, that's how it works! Oh, I can vacuum like crazy now! (*LEATRICE starts vacuuming; she works her way from the floor up to the long table behind the sofa where she manages to knock off a breakaway vase, which smashes to the floor. She turns off the machine. Both ladies look at the pieces, then at each other.*) It was an ugly old vase anyhow.

SYLVIA. It isn't anymore. Darling, there's a rule of thumb, never vacuum anything above your waist.

LEATRICE. All right, but I'll pay for it.

SYLVIA. What with, food—(*She stops herself.*) No, we're in a lifeboat. Here, I'll sweep up the little pieces. (*LEATRICE turns the machine back on again, working her way back along the drapes, lining the US. window. She vacuums the drapes, but down toward the bottom, about calf-length—nevertheless, the suction pulls them down and they fall to the floor with a thud. LEATRICE jumps back, turns off the machine. SYLVIA and LEATRICE survey the damage.*) Well, now, that's much better.

LEATRICE. They were below my waist!

SYLVIA. Darling, if you keep this up, the whole *apartment* will be below your waist. (*reaching for the vacuum cleaner*) Leatrice, why don't you let me finish that?

LEATRICE. (*clinging to it*) No, no, I just love to vacuum. I do. I can't explain it, but right now I have an urge to vacuum this whole apartment, "21," the balcony of the Shubert Theater and all five corners of your mind.

SYLVIA. I know you do. Sweetheart, I had a brother once who just loved to operate. Only one little problem — he wasn't a doctor. It's just that there's not a particularly good chemistry between you and this specific machine. Here . . . (*taking it*) Tidy up the drapes, do something *amusing* with them and I'll finish vacuuming. There's a dear. Now I'll show you how to clean house. I took lessons from Joan Crawford. (*SYLVIA, vacuuming from US.L., down past the mantel, turns and backs into the remaining stand-up lamp, knocking it down and breaking it. She turns off the machine, looks from one broken lamp to the other. She speaks with mock reverence.*) They were a pair in life—now they're together in death!

LEGENDS 71

LEATRICE. Perhaps we'd best not vacuum any more.

SYLVIA. Right. Let's just clean up the mess we made before and the one we made now. Do you know, I don't feel anything yet.

LEATRICE. Neither do I. Except I must say, breakage doesn't disturb me as much as it used to. I feel like it's . . . (*singing*) "Just one of those things, just one of those crazy things." (*LEATRICE plops down on the coffee table, the heels of her shoes down, her toes pointed up. She examines them in wonder, then reaches down and pushes her toes down to the floor.*)

SYLVIA. (*out of the blue*) You know what always burned me about you?

LEATRICE. What?

SYLVIA. Being an orphan.

LEATRICE. You were jealous of me being an orphan — whatever for?

SYLVIA. Well, it's so glamorous.

LEATRICE. Glamorous!

SYLVIA. And mysterious. All those rumors — Leatrice is a princess. Leatrice is a mulatto. Leatrice was found floating in a septic tank. Leatrice *is* the Lindberg baby!

LEATRICE. You made that one up.

SYLVIA. I did, I liked it.

LEATRICE. You know what? I think that's why I became an actress, I do. I thought, "I'll become a famous movie star and then my real parents will come forward and claim me." But they never did. (*then*) Maybe I'm still waiting.

SYLVIA. Didn't that just about kill you?

LEATRICE. Not after a while. I'd fantasized so much about who or what they could be — they couldn't possibly have lived up to my imagination. It did make me an actress. I was pretending so much every minute of every day about who I might be, I was just naturally playing "let's pretend," which led to doing it for a living. The other thing was: they could never nail down my real age.

SYLVIA. You're telling me! Incidentally, I happen to know your real age.

LEATRICE. (*quickly*) That's a lie!

SYLVIA. I didn't even say it.

LEATRICE. It's still a lie.

ARETHA. (*enters from the kitchen*) How're my movie stars doin'?

SYLVIA. Honey, we're fine. We cleaned up. We smashed a vase, knocked down a curtain and broke the other lamp.

ARETHA. You're frisky little devils, aren't you.

SYLVIA. And we don't feel a thing.

ARETHA. Well, supper's coming up in a jiffy. Ties and jackets for the gentlemen. Wigs for the ladies. And heavy tipping is encouraged. (*goes back into kitchen*)

SYLVIA. My mother!

LEATRICE. Your mother?

SYLVIA. I'll bet my mother's responsible for the whole loneliness thing.

LEATRICE. Funny, one never thinks of you ever having had a mother.

SYLVIA. Well, I did. You know something I remember about my mother?

LEATRICE. What?

SYLVIA. I always thought of it as just another childhood memory. But now, I'll just bet it started the whole loneliness thing. (*SYLVIA stares off into space in wonder. LEATRICE starts to get up from the coffee table, wobbles to chair and as she sits, her toes pop up again. She reacts and pushes them back down.*)

LEATRICE. Well, are you going to share it or just replay it in your own mind?

SYLVIA. No. No, you see, when I was about seven years old, my mother came into my room and caught me by surprise looking at my ass in a mirror. (*LEATRICE goes to SYLVIA and kneels by her chair.*) Well, you should have heard the excitement. She went straight to the telephone, called up my father at the office and said, "Frank, you won't believe what happened. I just caught Sylvia looking at her behind in a mirror!" Well, I couldn't see what all the excitement was about. I mean, it was my mirror and it was my ass and I wanted to see what it looked like. I wasn't doing anything to it. I was just looking at it. Well, my mother dragged me out to our fenced-in backyard, locked me in and told me to stay there. (*rises, staggers to the couch and collapses*) Jesus, I'm chatty. Maybe that stuff is working and I'm the chatty type. (*sits in wonderment for a while, then suddenly slaps her hands down on both thighs*) Well! (*Both ladies react in surprise.*) Along about six o'clock, I began to get cold and lonely, and cry. (*stands*) So I knocked on our back kitchen door and I said, "Mother, please, let me come in now, it's getting dark and I'm lonely." And she said: "Sylvia, you stay right there, you're going to be lonely most of your life, so you might as well get used to it."

LEATRICE. Ah-hah!

SYLVIA. Uh-huh. (*Both nod their heads.*) Well, when my father got home, they grilled me for about an hour. They seemed to feel that there was this club made up of little girls and we all got together and looked at our asses in our mirrors. When they finally let me go, I was so mad I ran up to the attic with a fly swatter and killed every last fly I could find. And then I spelled my whole name out in dead flies.

LEATRICE. (*standing*) You know something?

SYLVIA. What?

LEATRICE. I don't think I ever looked at my—behind.

SYLVIA. Never?

LEATRICE. Well, not that I remember. Certainly not with a mirror.

SYLVIA. Well, it would be extremely difficult to do it any other way (*LEATRICE attempts to look at her behind over one shoulder, then the other.*) No, I don't believe there's a civilized person in the entire world hasn't backed up to a mirror.

LEATRICE. (*mulling it over*) No, I don't think I ever did.

SYLVIA. You want me to have Aretha haul one out?

LEATRICE. Sylvia! (*then laughing*) Maybe later. (*Both laugh over this for some time. Then:*) What are we laughing at? (*standing*) Our careers?

SYLVIA. (*thinks for a moment*) No—asses! We've certainly known our share of those in our time, haven't we?

LEATRICE. (*crossing to sit next to SYLVIA on the sofa*) Speaking of that, whatever happened to Laura St. Clair?

SYLVIA. I heard she died of boredom while dictating her memoirs. (*They laugh again and flop around on the couch as ARETHA enters with a tray.*)

ARETHA. Chow down, my happy little lumberjacks! I've been hearing laughter. Such a sweet sound. Come along, ladies, put on the feedbag. I think the two of you are flying higher than a kite.

SYLVIA. Oh, Leatrice, I really think this play is so good. But then we always think every play we do is good. I don't suppose people ever actually get together and decide: "Let's put on a steaming turd!" Well, I don't suppose they do.

LEATRICE. Umm, my last play, *Bad Tidings*—Lord, was the author right on with that title. Anyhow, terrific cast, Otto What's-his-name, the other Hermione, Estelle Whosey—

SYLVIA. Wait a minute, you always remember everyone's—

LEATRICE. Not now I don't. I'm beginning to feel a little who-who. I'll be lucky if I can remember my address, I should be wearing dog-tags. We opened in Boston, the play was so complicated, *Variety* said it had more plots than a cemetery. Even the cast couldn't figure out who was doing what to whom, let alone why. But it had "language"—that's what we all fell in love with. Opening night in Boston there were so many people walking out we thought there was a fire in the theater. No fire, it was a ticking bomb they were fleeing. Every night we'd arrive for half hour and the stage doorman would actually throw our keys at us. By the end of the first week we had a summit meeting in the producer's suite at the Ritz. We'd all but decided to defuse the bomb, bury the show, when room service arrived in the form of this very elegant, well-spoken, sleek Italian waiter. While he's serving the shrimp cocktails, he recognized me and Otto What's-his-name and the other Hermione and said: "If you don't mind me saying, my wife and I saw your show the other night and we thought it was better than *Who's Afraid of Virginia Woolf.*" (*wipes her mouth with a napkin, goes on eating*) Well, that's what we thought when we read it. And that did it. We broke out the champagne, toasted the waiter *and* our brilliant show, whipped into New York and were practically stoned to death on opening night. Frank Rich said we should do the show in the Middle East, the Jews and Arabs would stop fighting each other and turn on us!

SYLVIA. You talk and eat at the same time better than anyone I ever met.

LEATRICE. Orphanage training, you had to eat fast or — nada!
SYLVIA. Oh, Leatrice, what do you say, let's do the play.
LEATRICE. If we could only do it when we're all fuzzy and friendly, like now.
SYLVIA. Maybe we could. We could knock back a brownie every night at half hour. Oh, Leatrice, if you're broke — I mean, I'm broke — what else is there to do but work? I always just pissed money away. I thought you were a pretty smart cookie with a buck, though.
LEATRICE. I always thought so, too.
SYLVIA. See, with me it was mostly husbands.
LEATRICE. Yes, dear, we know.
SYLVIA. It's supposed to work the opposite, but it didn't. I suppose I was just so irresistible I had to pay them to leave me alone.
LEATRICE. Either that or they demanded minimum wages for work already performed.
SYLVIA. That's my Leatrice. But you . . . ? Last I heard, you'd gone off to Europe. Well . . . ?
LEATRICE. Well, I'm deciding whether to tell you or not.
SYLVIA. Oh, go ahead. I'll tell you a secret, you tell me one. I'll tell you where my last bundle went. I put six hundred and fifty thousand dollars into a film to reactivate my own career. (*takes LEATRICE's hands*) It was unreleasable! (*almost near tears*) They couldn't even sell it to *cable*! My own money. And my Lila and grandchildren need it so . . . Oh, my God, I must have been mad! So there. And you?
LEATRICE. All right, I'll tell you. I went to France to do one of those pictures with an international cast — which means we all spoke our own language. My lawyer would

ask me a question in French, I'd answer in English, the prosecuting attorney would object in Swedish and the judge would overrule in German. I had no idea *what* was going on — but I fell in love with the author. French. Thirty-four, loved older women and guess what — *really* did. I still had some money then, a couple of hundred thousand, and he was making a good salary. But he wanted to open a restaurant and call it — Chez Leatrice. So we pooled our money, formed a French corporation and —

SYLVIA. Watch out for those.

LEATRICE. — We were looking for the right spot, when —

SYLVIA. Oh, God, Leatrice, is this going to be a sad story?

LEATRICE. Well, a true one.

SYLVIA. That's a sad one.

LEATRICE. One morning — oh, he was lovely in the mornings. He discovered a hard little lump under my right breast. It always amazed me that I didn't find it, it took a lover . . .

SYLVIA. Oh, Lord . . .

LEATRICE. When it was diagnosed, a Swiss clinic was recommended. One that guarantees secrecy. So Jean-Louis and I went to Switzerland where I underwent treatment for a year . . . no, a year and a half.

SYLVIA. Switzerland, so that's where you disappeared to. A year and a half in Switzerland. I never liked Switzerland.

LEATRICE. You were right, living in Switzerland is like living in a convent with a bunch of crooked nuns!

SYLVIA. But they treated you, you didn't have to —

LEATRICE. You know how we hang on to our careers? I had everything done — but December 21st — Merry

Christmas—I had a mastectomy. Jean-Louis went through it with me all the way. And when I asked him if it would affect his . . . ardor . . . seems an obvious question, but you have to ask it, don't you?

SYLVIA. Yes . . .

LEATRICE. He would always squeeze my hand and say, "No, no," but he never looked me in the eye. January 2nd—Happy New Year—he disappeared. He left me a bottle of champagne, a dozen red roses, a check for $20,000, and a note saying he was a coward, ashamed—

SYLVIA. Why didn't you go after him?

LEATRICE. (*standing*) Pride! Asinine pride. When you go through something like that, you're so raw. Also, I wanted, at all cost, for no one to know.

SYLVIA. But you just told *me*, of all people!

LEATRICE. That was two years ago. Also, I'm afraid we're drugged to the gills. There's an ever-so-slight rolling movement to this lifeboat now, and the sea is getting so choppy and the colors are so brilliant!

SYLVIA. (*stands, goes to her*) But even so . . . Oh, Leatrice—I'm sorry you had to go through all that, I am. You are one brave, beautiful—bitch! (*They both burst into laughter. The brownies are working. SYLVIA has embraced LEATRICE. Both exchange looks acknowledging this feeling is genuine.*) Here we are a couple of broken-down fillies—but still in the race, huh? (*The intercom buzzes.*)

LEATRICE. Mr. Klemmer—Oh, not now! Oh, son-of-a-bear!

SYLVIA. Aretha, if that's Mr.—and it just has to be—tell them to send him up now.

LEATRICE. No!

SYLVIA. Go ahead, Aretha.

LEATRICE. Why now?

SYLVIA. Because you're in a good mood.
LEATRICE. I was, but I'm not anymore.
SYLVIA. Well, when did it stop?
LEATRICE. When the bell rang!
SYLVIA. All right, then, but please, don't louse it up for me. If you're fool enough to turn down a play when you're on food stamps — let's just say that I'm available, but you've signed to play the tooth fairy in *The History Of Dental Hygiene*.
ARETHA. (on intercom) Yes . . . Mr. Klemmer . . . Well, send him right up.
LEATRICE. No!
SYLVIA. Yes!
ARETHA. Now listen, I heard everything you all said in here.
SYLVIA. Aretha!
ARETHA. Well, if you had two movie stars and they got into your brownies — wouldn't you be interested in the results? Now, if you don't take this offer after what I've heard, you are two of the dumbest white women I ever knew, and I've know some dummies! Now, get your act together, ladies, and do it in double time. Quick now . . . ! Or I'll spill the beans to *The Enquirer*!
SYLVIA. Hairbrushes!
LEATRICE. And a hand mirror.
SYLVIA. Leatrice, you're not going to check it out *now*!
LEATRICE. Oh, Sylvia! Wouldn't you know you'd get me into this kind of mess! I'm going to hide under the bed. (*going toward the bedroom*)
SYLVIA. You've been doing that for years! Leatrice, stop it! Come on, we need the work, we need the money, we need the — do you know what a star can make on Broadway now?
LEATRICE. (*strong*) I don't care about all that! I don't

care at all! (*sudden change of tone*) How much?

SYLVIA. Eight, ten, twelve thousand dollars a week. Wait a minute, don't tell me you're nervous.

LEATRICE. Of course I'm nervous!

SYLVIA. What's to be nervous, he wants us, doesn't he?

LEATRICE. I don't know!

SYLVIA. Of course he does. Aretha, pour us some coffee, please, black.

ARETHA. I will, if you tell me whose apartment this is and who it is I work for, you, Miss Monsée, Mrs. Coulter or Imelda Marcos.

SYLVIA. It doesn't make any difference, just serve like a dream and help us if we have trouble walking or talking or even crawling.

ARETHA. Gotcha!

SYLVIA & LEATRICE. How do I look?—Terrific!

SYLVIA. Now . . . redember . . .

LEATRICE. Redember?

SYLVIA. Whatever he offers—ask for more. (*The doorbell rings.*) Now, let's sit down and compose ourselves . . . (*LEATRICE sits in extreme* S.R. *chair; SYLVIA sits in chair next to her. LEATRICE's toes are pointed up again. This time, SYLVIA get up and pushes them back down—she sits again.*) Judas Priest! I forgot all about billing! Leatrice, I know you—you wouldn't try to screw me, would you?

LEATRICE. Of course not, darling.

SYLVIA. Thank you.

LEATRICE. My agent will do that.

SYLVIA. Now, it's an acting exercise! We won't act drugged, act normal.

ARETHA. (*offstage; as the door opens*) Hello . . . you must be—

MARTIN. (offstage) Martin Klemmer, producer of the Off-Broadway hit, *Craps!*
ARETHA. (*offstage*) Let me take your coat.
MARTIN. (*offstage*) Thank you. No, I'll keep this.
ARETHA. (*offstage*) Right this way. Martin Klemmer, producer of the Off-Broadway hit, *Craps!*?

(*MARTIN KLEMMER, beautifully dressed, carrying a handsome briefcase, enters behind ARETHA.*)

MARTIN. Please, excuse me. I wouldn't have kept you waiting for anything, but I had a very important meeting—(*LEATRICE turns her chair to KLEMMER.*) Oh, my God! (*SYLVIA does the same.*) Oh, *my God!*
SYLVIA. What?
MARTIN. Time has stood still for the two of you. (*Offers his hand; SYLVIA takes it, struggles to get up.*) Miss Glenn, don't get up.
SYLVIA. (*grateful, falling back into her chair*) Oh, thank you.
MARTIN. (*extending his hand to her*) Miss Monsée.
LEATRICE. (*takes it, keeps shaking it*) It's so nice to meet you. Sylvia's having the apartment redembered.
ARETHA. (*quickly*) She means—redone.
MARTIN. (*working his hand free*) A double pleasure.
SYLVIA. May we offer you a drink?
MARTIN. No, thank you. I really don't drink.
LEATRICE. Neither do I. How 'bout a gin-on-the-rocks?
MARTIN. Maybe a little Perrier. Again, I'm sorry I'm late, but I have got some splendid news.
SYLVIA. Well, Leatrice and I have been discussing the play. And we've come to the firm conclusion that—

what? (*losing her point, turning to LEATRICE*)

LEATRICE. That—uh—we like it. But we're not all that anxious to—uh—Would you like a brownie?

MARTIN. No, thank you. I gotta watch my tumtum.

SYLVIA. By the way, the address where you sent the script is more like an office that I keep over on the West . . .

MARTIN. Save it, Miss Glenn. I'm aware of your circumstances, both of you. (*crosses* S.L. *to the coffee table*) I tried to do a Dunn & Bradstreet check on you and you weren't even listed. How can life be so cruel to such charming ladies? (*He puts his briefcase down on the coffee table as ARETHA enters with a glass of Perrier.*) Now, would you do me one little favor? Forget Paul Newman!

ALL THREE LADIES. Forget Paul Newman!

MARTIN. His film in Northern Sumatra, it's way behind schedule and he doesn't know when he'll be free. (*sits in chair,* S.L.) But I have a clothing manufacturer who needs a tax write-off right now. He's willing to put up $250,000.—

LEATRICE. $250,000!

SYLVIA. You can't do a play for that now, unless you do it in your . . .

LEATRICE. . . . kitchen.

SYLVIA. Thank you, dear.

MARTIN. (*Standing and walking* US. *to pick up a chair by the window, which he brings down, places between the two ladies and sits. He holds some papers in his hand.*) For $250,000—with concessions on all parts—we can open at the Lucille Lortel, the old Theatre de Lys, one of the best Off-Broadway houses—

SYLVIA & LEATRICE. Off-Broadway?

MARTIN. Hear me out, please. (*By this time, he's sit-*

ting between them.) We could go into rehearsal at the end of the month—open four weeks later. The theater seats 299. I would announce a limited engagement of ten weeks, so we'd be sure to pack 'em in, especially with the two of you. Favored nations clause all around—equal, equal. You'd each get $672.50 per week.

LEATRICE. Six hundred and seventy-two fifty!

SYLVIA. And a tax write-off indicates the backer is looking for a flop!

MARTIN. No, no! We will not have a flop. The play is terrific entertainment. There is a vast audience that'll pay just to see you sit on the same stage together, let alone rip each other's heads off. Now, if the play is a hit, we move uptown—Broadway! Your contracts convert at that time and you each get eight thousand dollars a week. Now, here is a complete fact sheet for each, and a contract for each, including the conversion clause.

SYLVIA. Six hundred and seventy-two fifty a week?

LEATRICE. No out-of-town tryout?

MARTIN. Ninety-six previews.

SYLVIA & LEATRICE. Ninety-six previews!

MARTIN. By far the best way to do this. It's a first play by an unknown author. Let the critics discover him. God, they love to do that. See, with the two of you, we have built-in publicity. The only way I can see a disaster is in case of a nuclear attack. (*MARTIN giggles. ARETHA picks up on it and laughs out loud. He joins in and laughs even louder.*) Here is a list of seven directors who've read the play. Five want to do it—in the event you both agree.

SYLVIA. You mean two refused?

MARTIN. No, no, no. One has a film starting in January and the other has a minor heart condition. His doctor advised him that working with the two of you would be extremely hazardous. Here—and God forbid it should ever come to this—is a list of other actresses who are distinct possibilities in the event you should refuse the project.

SYLVIA. (*not at all pleased*) Other actresses? On second thought, why *don't* you have a brownie? They're absolutely delicious.

MARTIN. You know, I don't mind if I do. I haven't had a bite to eat all day. (*As he places two lists of actresses on the chair between the ladies, ARETHA, who is standing US. of the table which backs the sofa, picks up the plate of brownies and, without looking at MARTIN, holds it out toward him. She raises her other hand and checks her watch—a comic countdown for the brownie blastoff. As he jams a brownie in his mouth:*) Now, I have given the play to none of them—so far. However, I have already placed a deposit on the theater—(*takes another brownie*)—I'm posting my Equity bond tomorrow. (*to ARETHA*) Good God, these are out of this world!

ARETHA. That's it! (*SYLVIA and LEATRICE, who have been eyeing the lists, now pick them up from the chair.*)

MARTIN. So, in the event either or both of you should decline—I must move swiftly in other directions.

SYLVIA. (*reading from the list*) Elizabeth Taylor.

LEATRICE. Debbie Reynolds.

SYLVIA. Say, there's a pair. (*turning to MARTIN*) Perhaps you could get Eddie Fisher for the man's part.

LEATRICE. Lana Turner.

SYLVIA. I thought we took care of her.

LEATRICE. June Allyson.

SYLVIA. Oh, she'd play *your* part.

LEATRICE. Shelley Winters.

SYLVIA. No comment.

MARTIN. (*crossing to stand above the empty chair*) I can't tell you the excitement this script is stirring up all over town. I've already gotten calls from all the Gabors and half the Redgraves.

SYLVIA. Ginger Rogers. Ginger *Rogers*!

LEATRICE. She still plays tennis.

SYLVIA. So does John McEnroe! (*then*) Arlene Dahl.

LEATRICE. Rhonda Fleming.

SYLVIA. (*looking up, thoughtfully*) Aren't they the same one?

MARTIN. (*sitting on the chair between them*) Look, as I said before, I know your circumstances, both of you. I don't want to dwell on this aspect, only to let you know that I'm aware. I don't feel I'm taking advantage. I'm being candid with you. I will do everything in my power to assure the best possible production. Now, here is a list—(*MARTIN stands, beginning to cross to the coffee table. As he crosses, he does a funny little hop-skip-head-and-shoulder jerk. The brownie has started. He is completely amazed by what he's done. For a second, he freezes and looks behind him to see if he can figure out what happened. After a second, he walks very self-consciously and wooden to his briefcase.*)—Now, here's a list for your approval of other actors who could play the male lead. (*He returns to sit between them once again, handing them each a sheet of paper.*) Now, I'm not naive enough to believe you'd each sign your contract right now. It would be sheer folly of me to try to back either one of you two ladies into a corner. I do not believe in pressuring anyone, especially in this business. (*During the following sentence, he moves both hands back and forth in front of him from side to side until they finally work up to the top of his head where his hands have become like two huge ears.*) I know you have your agents and your lawyers, your accountants and your managers and your doidies and your doidies— (*He freezes, amazed at his behavior. He brings his hands slowly down to his lap, trying to pull himself together.*)—Uh, but I would like to have a definite yes or no within five days. That would be by Monday afternoon at three. (*He stands carefully.*) I won't be staying much longer. (*He picks up the chair and, very stiffly, in a bent-down position carries it back to where he got it originally. After setting it down, he walks back to the ladies, clears his throat and straightens his tie.*) Now, I want you to know I'm not going to do a hard sell. (*dipping his hands and his knees left, right and left, like he's doing the "twist"*) No way, no way, no way! (*catches himself and pulls himself together*) I know you have minds of your own. I know even more that you realize what this play could mean to your careers at this particular time, to say nothing of your finances. (*He pokes his index finger into LEATRICE's stomach and makes a buzzing sound.*) Zzzzzzz! (*He pulls back his finger in horror and crosses quickly to the coffee table. As he walks away, LEATRICE rises to her full height.*)

LEATRICE. Mr. Klemmer, we were not rich because we were famous.

SYLVIA. Famous because we were rich.

LEATRICE. Right. But because of whom we were.

SYLVIA. Are.

LEATRICE. Right again. (*sits abruptly. MARTIN, who stands S.L. of the coffee table facing them, begins to speak completely tongue-tied in double-talk.*)

MARTIN. When the cran-a-stan farble-stoff in the riber trong . . . (*He stops himself, trying to get his tongue to work right, and gives it another try.*) Perform-a-ding in the rabble-dorf needs a derma-drang . . . (*Completely embarrassed by his behavior, he stands in silence for a moment, while the two ladies stare at him intently. Then he bows his head three times while speaking in baby talk.*) I'm torry, I'm torry, I'm torry.

SYLVIA. (*regarding him and speaking in all seriousness as she turns to LEATRICE*) By God, Leatrice, I think he has a point there.

MARTIN. (*picking up the briefcase and starting to walk back to them*) Thank you for your time and consideration and I hope the prospect of a long and — (*a wild little hand wave and high voice*) — happy association — (*back to normal*) — working as well as personal is not just a wishful fantasy on my part. Miss Monsée, I have a video cassette of your performance in *Rainbow's End*, an all-time Academy Award favorite. (*He places the palm of his hand against her nose and makes a honking sound. Trying to pull himself together, he turns to SYLVIA.*) And Miss Glenn . . . (*gets down on his knees by her chair*) . . . I have you in *Go For Broke*. My God, you were simply brilliant! (*He puts his right hand between her legs at about calf-length and wiggles it wildly back and forth while making a turkey gobbling noise: "Gobble, gobble, gobble, gobble!" He stands up in absolute horror, clears his throat.*) Uh . . . didn't you also win an Oscar for that?

SYLVIA. Why, yes, I did.

LEATRICE. (*swatting at MARTIN with the list she holds in her hand*) She played a hooker. And she was absolutely marvelous!

MARTIN. (*turning to SYLVIA*) I can believe it. Still on the job, huh? (*starts to laugh, stops himself immediately*) Oh, in the event you decide not to do the play, be assured all of your financial information goes to the grave with me. Also, if you should decline, I'd be most honored to have you as my guests on opening night so you could enjoy the play and whoever the hell else is in it! (*starts to back* US. *on his way out*) Again, it's lovely to see you both looking so well . . . you're obviously getting along . . . (*His wave is suddenly transformed into a "jerking off" motion*) . . . thank you for your time and your trouble and — wow! (*Completely giving in to the brownies, he skips madly down to LEATRICE's chair, sits on the edge of it and leans back as if he'd passed out.*) Wow! (*LEATRICE fans his face with the sheets she holds. He soon pulls himself together and sits up.*) Whee! (*English accent*) Might I share this moment with you? (*back to his own voice as he gives LEATRICE a little pinch on the thigh*) You know something, I'd hoped to take the two of you out to a little din-din. But, get this, you'll love it, I used to be an actor before I produced my Off-Broadway crap, *Hits*. (*MARTIN covers his face with his hands as if to erase his mistake.*) Anyway, one of my lead actors is sick. (*He pantomimes drinking from a bottle, making "glug, glug, glug" sounds.*) You got it. So — (*standing*) — I'm going to have to go on tonight in the lead. I won't even have time for dinner myself.

ARETHA. (*as she picks up the plate of brownies and holds it out*) Well, in that case, why don't you take a few more for the road?

MARTIN. (*walking to her and stuffing two or three more brownies in his mouth*) You're *too* kind. Don't mind if I do.

SYLVIA. Yes, by all means, and break a leg.

MARTIN. Goodbye. (*Then pretending to fall down, he limps for a second, then recovers.*) Just kidding, just kidding. So long, ladies. (*As he leaves, he trips on the landing leading to the foyer, then turns and steps right into the edge of the wall, seeming to smash his face against it. He roars with laughter and exits.*)

SYLVIA. (*rising, crossing Left, good-naturedly*) That son-of-a-bitch.

LEATRICE. (*stands*) Blackmailing, low-life killer.

ARETHA. Just look at the two of you. What are you fussing about? You just got a wild offer out of the blue. What else have you got to do? What on earth do you want?

LEATRICE. I want yesterday.

ARETHA. Well, you're not getting it, they sold it.

SYLVIA. I know what I don't want. I don't want to end up all lonely and forgotten and go to sleep in a cramped studio apartment with a lighted cigarette in my hand. I mean, I want to be cremated, but I don't want to do it myself. (*sits on sofa*)

LEATRICE. Or just get old and shriveled up, and then you take a bath, pull the plug and down the drain you go. (*She flops into a chair toward* C.S.)

SYLVIA. Like Gloria Swanson. She got tinier and tinier.

LEATRICE. She did, didn't she?

SYLVIA. Toward the end, she could run under a coffee table with a picture hat on.

ARETHA. Then what in the name of Loretta H. Young are you whimperin' about! Take the bait and run with it. You got enough energy to tear up this whole apartment, why don't you get up onstage and tear *it* up? You need to take that negative energy and turn it into something positive and make something good happen.

LEATRICE. Sylvia, let's do the play! We'd be doing what we know how to do. No — what we love to do!

SYLVIA. Oh, Lord — thank you for bringing her to her senses. (*then*) Let's give 'em the funhouse, the roller coaster *and* the parachute ride! Let's give 'em a show they'll never forget.

LEATRICE. We'll give 'em our charisma.

SYLVIA. We'll give 'em our feud, they'll remember that.

LEATRICE. And if they don't, we'll remind them.

ARETHA. You should, because people love to get in on that shit. (*She exits into the kitchen.*)

LEATRICE. Sylvia . . . you know after spending an evening with you — and surviving — I think there's actually a very sweet person way deep down inside you absolutely screaming to get out. I do. And I think your public would like to see that person.

SYLVIA. Why, thank you, Leatrice.

LEATRICE. What if we really surprise them and switch parts, you could play the goody-goody for a change.

SYLVIA. Say, I'd get to cry and then in Act II, when you throw acid in my face, I'd get all that sympathy. Of course, the mean one, Cornelia, does have a lot more to say.

LEATRICE. Remember, darling, what whosey-whatsit said, "There are no small parts, there are only small actors." Of course, if we did switch, I'd have to play the bitch for the first time in my life. (*suddenly*) Oh, hot-diggety-dog! (*then sweetly*) I wonder if I could do it?

SYLVIA. Darling, remember, I've spent an evening with you, too. You'll be absolutely purr-fect.

LEATRICE. (*picking up SYLVIA's script which is on an end table near sofa, opening to a page*) But I'd have to read lines like — well, like this? (*really knocking them out*) "Cathy, you've seen so many ceilings in Hollywood, they're starting to call you Michael-Angela." Then you say, "Blah, blah, blah, blah, blah, blah, blah." And I say, "Every major star ought to have a telethon, you could do one for *bedsores*!" (*sweetly again*) You really think I bring it off?

SYLVIA. You bet I do.

LEATRICE. Oh, what fun! Then we'll switch?

SYLVIA. What the hell, why not?

LEATRICE. Is that a promise?

SYLVIA. Cross my heart and hope to die.

LEATRICE. Oh, good. You see, I have to tell you one teensy tiny little secret.

SYLVIA. I don't know why teensy tiny always makes me nervous, but it does.

LEATRICE. Now, Sylvia. You see, I'd already decided to do the play way before I even got here tonight.

SYLVIA. (*gasping*) Why, you little . . . !

LEATRICE. It was just a matter of getting the role I wanted and I just got it!

SYLVIA. Oh, Leatrice, I always knew you were rotten to the core. (*Then she laughs.*) We're going to have such a good time.

LEATRICE. (*getting her cape and purse*) Just think — we'll have somewhere to go in the evenings.

SYLVIA. And get to wear costumes and put on makeup. And the press will eat us up. Let's face it, at this moment, we're faced with a shortage of one of our greatest natural resources — dirt. And that's what we'll give 'em — dirt!

LEATRICE. And we won't have to wait to be invited to a party, we'll be throwing the party every night. (*reaching out her arms*) Give us a kiss.

SYLVIA. (*as they embrace*) Oh, I can't wait for opening night, can you?

LEATRICE. No . . . (*walking to the foyer*) And do you know why, darling?

SYLVIA. Why, angel?

LEATRICE. (*striking a pose*) Because, sweetheart, *I'm going to mop up the stage with you!* (*She blows a kiss and exits. SYLVIA, hooting with laughter, walks up to the hallway platform.*)

SYLVIA. Oh, I always did love your sense of humor. (*She waits for a reply. Then:*) Leatrice, you were kidding, weren't you? (*Sound of front door slamming, SYLVIA's hands go to her face as she turns around.*) Oh, son-of-a-bear!

BLACKOUT

CURTAIN

PROP PRESET

ACT ONE

Scene 1

MARTIN KLEMMER'S OFFICE

1. Air conditioner in s.r. window
2. File cabinet
3. Two bookcases (one on either side of door)
4. Desk
    a. One touch tone telephone
    b. One speaker
    c. One small legal pad
    d. One coffee mug with water in it
    e. One pencil
    f. One flower pot with dead plant
    g. One legal pad
    h. One pen in stand
    i. One script
    j. Various papers
5. Swivel chair with pillow
6. Various scripts, papers, books and office equipment on book shelves and on file cabinet
7. Show poster for "Craps"
8. Various black & white show pictures on wall

Scene 2

DOROTHY COULTER'S APARTMENT

1. Oriental side table ds.r. (s.r. of easy chair and ottoman)
    a. One plate of brownies covered with cellophane

b. One silver decorative box
   c. One vase of white cyclamens under table
2. One standing lamp US. of oriental side table
   a. Draped with party decorations
3. One magazine rack on floor (on stage side of DS.R. chair)
   a. Time, Newsweek & Harpers in rack
   Note: Address stickers on magazines
      Mrs. Dorothy Coulter
      758 Park Ave.
      New York City, N. Y. 10021
4. One bar (in front of #2 S.R. window)
   a. One Kodak Instamatic X15F flash camera (set to take two photos)
   b. Two Bombay gin bottles filled with water
   c. Six cocktail glasses
   d. Small tray for glasses
   e. One stack of cocktail napkins
   f. One ice bucket with four plastic ice cubes
   g. One set of ice tongs
   h. One small plate with lime wedges
   i. One vase of flowers
5. One green baby grand piano US.C. keyboard facing S.R.
   a. Shawl draped over piano
   b. Five helium balloons on weighted string
   c. One statuette (US. end of keyboard)
   d. Four framed autographed photos to Dorothy Coulter
      1. Imelda Marcos
      2. Mayor Koch
      3. Two from anyone
   e. One standing mirror

A galley
6. Sofa & sofa table (sofa table is attached to sofa on wagon that swings US. for Producer & Subway Units)
    a. Two throw pillows on sofa
    On Sofa Table:
    a. One telephone on S.L. end with cord long enough to reach sofa center
    b. One letter opener with pin attached to end to puncture balloons
    c. One small framed photo facing US.
    d. Two wrapped gifts
    e. (Fur coat draped over S.L. end — wardrobe)
7. Two swivel chairs on S.R. in between DS.R. chair and sofa
8. Two end tables — one on either end of sofa
    a. Table lamps on each table
    b. Five helium balloons on weighted string on S.L. table
9. One straight back chair against wall between piano and foyer
10. One Chippendale chair DS.L.
11. One round end table US. of Chippendale chair
12. One wing back chair DS.L. in alcove
13. Fireplace unit in S.L. wall
    a. Fireplace screen
    b. Fireplace equipment US. of unit
    On Mantle:
    a. One small photo
    b. One standing mirror (smaller than one on piano)
    c. One standing crucifix
14. Oil painting of Mrs. Coulter — must be able to be easily struck by Sylvia

96   LEGENDS

15. One china cabinet built into US.L. wall filled with books, china and objects d'art
15a. Intercom phone on wall
16. One two drawer antique chest below china cabinet
    a. One large Chinese vase with gladioli (US. end)
    b. Stone head of Budda (center)
17. One coffee table centered DS. of sofa
    a. Two large platters heaping with finger sandwiches and covered with cellophane and decorated with ribbons
18. One standing lamp DS. of bedroom door against S.L. wall
    a. Draped with party decorations
19. One small waste can between bar and piano against wall
20. FAREWELL DEAR ARETHA banner hanging from ceiling beam (Must be rigged to come down with a yank on string from either end)
    a. Crepe wedding bells attached to either end
21. US.C. drape must be rigged to fall on cue

STAGE RIGHT PROP SET UP

1. One aluminum step ladder with four rungs   (Aretha)
2. One plate of canapes (smoked salmon and cavier)   (Aretha)
3. One empty saucer   (Aretha)
4. One plate of cheese and crackers   (Aretha)
5. One large frying pan   (Aretha)
6. Two bunches of five helium balloons on weighted strings   (Aretha)

STAGE LEFT PROP SET UP

1. One garment bag   (Sylvia)
2. One matching overnight bag with five framed photographs in it
     a. One Lana Turner   (Sylvia)
     b. One small Lila
     c. Three of any one
3. Ghetto blaster with batteries and blank tape   (Stripper)
4. Leatrice's purse with unemployment letter it   (Leatrice)
5. Script case with script in it   (Leatrice)
6. Telegram   (Stripper)
7. Business card   (Stripper)
8. Door slam by stage manager's desk
9. Sound booth
     a. Telephone on music stand
     b. Music stand for script

ACT TWO

Scene 1

SUBWAY SCENE

1. One orange trash can with debris S.R. corner
2. One unit with three pay phones
     a. Four quarters in S.L. phone coin return
     b. Empty Coca-Cola can on top of unit
     c. "Times Square" sign S.L.
     d. "No Litter on tracks" sign S.R.

Scene 2

DOROTHY COULTER'S APARTMENT

1. Overturn ottoman
2. Change lamp shade on D.R. lamp for a bent one and lay on seat of S.R. swivel chair with base toward DS.R. chair
3. On bar
   a. Strike used glasses, wash and return them
   b. Set empty, open Coke can with opaque glass
   c. Strike all props other than original bar set up
4. On piano
   a. Set Leatrice's wig on statuette
   b. Put Spanish shawl back on piano
5. Under piano
   a. Stack photos—place standing mirror on top

A galley
6. Put magazines back in rack
7. The C.S. swivel chair is facing US.
8. Bread crumbs are scattered about (esp. DS. between swivels)
9. Strike everything from sofa table except photo, which is face down and telephone. On S.R. end place Stripper's cape.
10. Place radio US. of sofa
11. Piece of Sylvia's dress is draped over DS. and iron
12. Script case on SR. end of coffee table with ice bag on top
13. Two sofa pillows on floor DS. of coffee table. The SR. pillow has the smashed Lana Turner photo under it.
14. Chippendale chair and end table are moved to Act II spikes

15. Breakaway lamp S.L. moved to Act II spikes and attached to floor.
16. Sylvia's wig is placed on top of S.L. lamp
17. On wing back chair S.L.
    a. Leatrice's cape, purse and gloves
18. Open US.L. window
19. Strike plate of cheese and crackers

STAGE RIGHT PROP SET UP

1. One bowl of fruit with spoon   (Aretha)
2. One silver tray: (Aretha)
    a. Two bowls of chili
    b. Two teaspoons wrapped in napkins
3. One cocktail glass with club soda in it   (Aretha)

STAGE LEFT PROP SET UP

1. One Policeman's ticket pad   (Policeman)
2. One ball point pen   (Policeman)
3. One small spiral notebook with spiral on top   (Policeman)
4. One vacuum cleaner—practical and hard wired (Controlled from stage manager desk)   (Aretha)
5. One dust pan and small broom   (Sylvia)
6. One briefcase   (Klemmer)
    a. One list of male movie stars
    b. One file folder
        1. Two sets of fact sheets and contracts
        2. Two sets of lists of other actresses
        3. One copy of list of directors
    c. Copy of Variety
7. Two hair brushes and hand mirror in bedroom   (Aretha)

PROP INVENTORY

DOROTHY COULTER'S APARTMENT

1 carpet with Oriental rug sewn in
5 oil paintings in frames
1 wing back chair
1 straight back chair with arms
1 round side table
1 floor lamp — breakaway
1 floor lamp with two shades — one good, one bent
fireplace screen and fireplace tools
1 two drawer chest — blonde
2 dark walnut end tables
2 table lamps with white shades
1 sofa with sofa table attached on castered wagon
1 black coffee table
1 swivel chair, matching sofa
1 oatmeal colored swivel chair
1 print upholstered arm chair with ottoman
8 drapes — one rigged to breakaway
1 green baby grand piano with piano bench
1 green oriental side table
1 wooden chest with doors and 1 drawer — (Bar)
1 waste basket
3 wooden African masks — in foyer
1 straight back chair
1 "Farewell Dear Aretha" banner
1 telephone with 15' cord
2 Bombay gin bottles
1 tray
2 empty Coke cans
1 pink glass
1 Chinese vase with flowers

LEGENDS

1 plate of brownies
1 silver decorative box
1 vase with white cyclamens
2 paper lays — party decorations
2 paper bells — party decorations
2 large paper bells with streamers — each end of banner
1 magazine rack
Time, Newsweek, Harpers with Coulter address on them
1 Kodak Instamatic X15F camera
flash bars for camera
6 cocktail glasses
stack of cocktail napkins
1 ice bucket
1 set ice tongs
1 small plate for lime wedges
1 ornamental vase with flowers
1 embroidered shawl for piano
numerous #10 latex balloons
4 strings with weights on one end for balloons
1 statuette for piano
9 framed photos
    a. Imelda Marcos
    b. Mayor Koch
    c. Lana Turner
    d. Lila
    e. five of anyone
2 standing mirrors — 1 large, one small
2 throw pillows for sofa
1 letter opener with pin attached
2 wrapped gifts
1 standing crucifix
1 oil painting of Dorothy Coulter
1 intercom — wall mount
1 stone head of budda

2 large platters heaping with finger sandwiches covered
   with cellophane
1 aluminum step ladder with four rungs
1 plate of canapes
1 small plate
1 plate of cheese and crackers
1 large frying pan
1 garment bag
1 matching overnight bag
1 "ghetto blaster"
1 unemployment letter to Leatrice Monsée
1 leather script case — large
1 telegram to Aretha
1 business card — Stripper
1 door slam
2 music stands — sounds booth
smashed Lana Turner photo
1 ice bag
1 piece of Sylvia's 2nd Act I dress
stale bread for crumbs
1 large tank of helium with balloon attachment
1 bowl of fruit
1 silver tray
2 bowls of chili
2 napkins
2 soup spoons
1 policeman's pad
1 ball point pen
1 small spiral notebook — spiral on top
1 portable vacuum cleaner — hardwired on
1 dust pan
1 small broom
1 briefcase

LEGENDS

1 list of male movie stars
2 sets of lists of other actresses
1 list of directors
1 copy of Variety
2 hairbrushes
1 hand mirror
Misc. books, figurines, etc. as dressing for china cabinet and bookcases

SUBWAY STATION

4 quarters
1 "Times Square" sign
1 "No Litter on Tracks" sign
1 orange trash can
1 empty Coke can

MARTIN KLEMMER'S OFFICE

1 file cabinet
2 small book cases
1 desk
1 touch tone telephone
1 small legal pad
1 coffee mug with water
1 pencil
1 flower pot with dead plant
1 pen in stand
1 script — "Star Wars"
swivel chair with pillow
Misc. books, papers and office equipment
"CRAPS" show poster
Various black & white production photos for wall

BOXES, ETC.

2 hampers
2 large furniture boxes
1 piano box
1 large box for hand props
2 refrigerators
4 cots
1 F.O.H. Equity Board
2 change of cast boards

WARDROBE INVENTORY

SYLVIA

1. one black fox fling
2. one pair red shoes
3. one black lizard purse
4. one red suit
5. three silver lamé dresses (one ripped ACT II)
6. one large dowager type necklace
7. one pair black gauntlets
8. one ivory Charmeuse dressing gown
9. one pair ivory t-strap shoes
10. one pair silver t-strap shoes
11. four rhinestone expandable arm bracelets
12. three wigs

LEATRICE

1. one tan fur cape
2. one new black dress with embroidery
3. one black fur cape
4. one black dress, Mackie
5. one black dress, Sansappellc
6. one black hat
7. three wigs

ARETHA

1. two grey maid's dresses
2. two maid's aprons
3. two maid's caps
4. one pair white shoes
5. one watch
6. one blue dress

7. one slip
8. one pair blue shoes
9. one fur coat (no sleeves)
10. one pair earrings
11. one hair flower

KLEMMER

1. one blue suit
2. two white shirts
3. two ties
4. one belt
5. one pair brown shoes
6. one grey jacket
7. one grey trousers
8. two yellow shirts
9. one pair tan shoes
10. two pocket squares
11. five pair yellow socks
12. seven pair blue socks
13. 14 t-shirts
14. one brown tweed overcoat with belt

POLICEMAN

1. one police jacket with fur collar
2. two police shirts
3. one pair navy-blue slacks
4. one black belt
5. one black gun belt with handcuffs and gun
6. one pair black shoes
7. one black tie
8. seven black pair socks
9. seven t-shirts
10. one police hat

11. one badge
12. one nameplate
13. one insignia

YOUNG MAN

1. two black shirts with white tux fronts
2. two white vests
3. two white collars with bow ties
4. one black cape with red lining
5. one black tail coat
6. three pair leopard print bikinis
7. two pair pink/black boxers
8. one G-string
9. one moon and star
10. one pair black boots
11. two white scarfs
12. one black top hat
13. one pair breakaway tux pants with red suspenders
14. one pair tux pants
15. seven brown pair socks

SYLVIA UNDERSTUDY

1. one red Dynasty suit
2. one silver dress with detachable train
3. one ivory dressing gown
4. one pair red shoes
5. one pair ivory shoes
6. one pair silver shoes

LEATRICE UNDERSTUDY

1. one black dress
2. one black pair shoes

3. one black hat
4. one pair earrings
5. one necklace
6. one wig

POLICEMAN UNDERSTUDY

1. one policeman jacket
2. one policeman shirt
3. one navy-blue pants
4. one pair black shoes
5. two t-shirts
6. two pair socks

YOUNG MAN UNDERSTUDY

1. one pair breakaway tux pants with suspenders
2. one pair tux pants
3. one G-string
4. one pair black boots
5. one top hat
6. one rehearsal shirt
7. one rehearsal jacket

ARETHA UNDERSTUDY

1. one blue sequinned dress
2. one pair blue shoes
3. one black slip
4. one green maid's dress with two collars
5. one maid's apron
6. one maid's hat
7. one pair green shoes
8. one wig

KLEMMER UNDERSTUDY

1. one pair blue jeans
2. one black bomber jacket
3. one blue shirt
4. one pair grey Reeboks
5. one grey three piece suit
6. one white shirt
7. one black belt
8. one yellow tie
9. one ascot
10. one yellow pocket square

DEAD COSTUMES

ARETHA:
1 grey maid's dress
six maid's collars
four maid's aprons
three maid's hats
two black maid's dresses
one "old" blue sequinned tent
one large black slip
1 silver purse
1 pair silver shoes

SYLVIA UNDERSTUDY:
two silver dresses
one red suit

LEATRICE UNDERSTUDY
two brown hats
one brown purse
one tan slip

one brocade jacket (ripped)
one brocade jacket (ACT I)
one beige chiffon dress

LEATRICE:
one beige chiffon dress
one brown suit
one tan skirt
one full tan slip
two silk brocade blouses
two tan brocade jackets (ACT I & II)
two brown brocade jackets (ACT I & II)

KLEMMER:
one burgundy bomber jacket
one pair jeans
two blue shirts
one pair grey trousers
one pair creme trousers
one brown sports coat
two ties
one pr. brown shoes

EARL:
two tux shirts
one cummerbund
one bow tie
one pair gloves
one burgundy brocade tux jacket
one pair tux shoes
one G-string
two pair white gloves

HAIR SUPPLIES

1. 1 bonnet hair dryer
2. 1 blow dryer
3. misc. rollers, hair pins, hair clips, T pins
4. curling iron
5. wig caps

WARDROBE SUPPLIES

1. 1 iron & ironing board
2. 1 steamer
3. 2 clothes brushes
4. shoe polishing kit
5. stripper tape
6. sleeve board
7. 1 pair knee pads

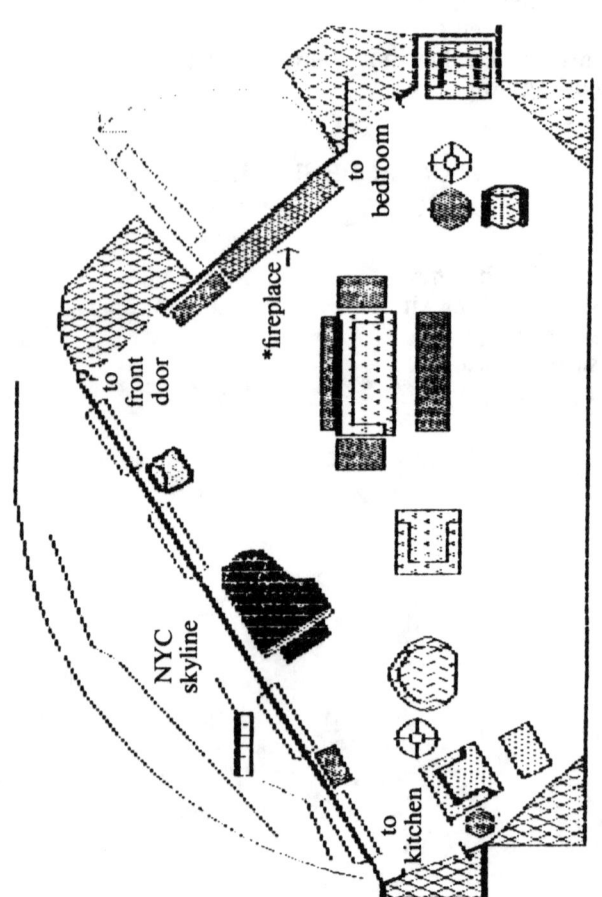

*Note: Fireplace flat is hinged to permit passage of Producer & Subway units.

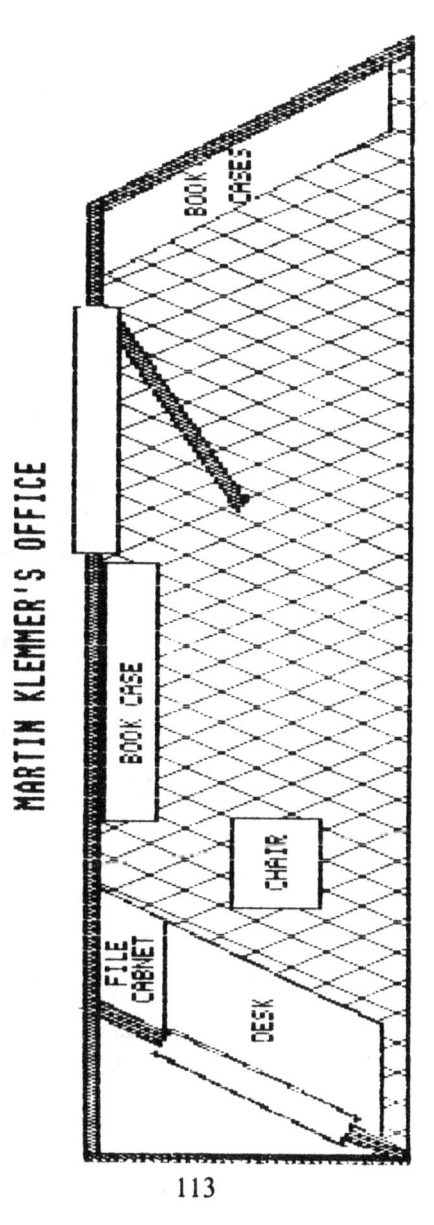

ACT I - SCENE 1
MARTIN KLEMMER'S OFFICE

SUBWAY SCENE
ACT II - SCENE 1

About the Playwright
JAMES KIRKWOOD

Born in California of acting parents, Lila Lee and James Kirkwood Sr., James Kirkwood started out as an actor, nightclub comedian, (as half of the team of Kirkwood and Goodman) disc jockey, etc. etc. At a quirky moment in his career, he sat down and wrote an autobiographical novel about his childhood, *There Must Be a Pony!* Later he dramatized this for the stage, starring Myrna Loy. Even later it was adapted as a TV film, starring Elizabeth Taylor. Thus began his writing career, although he continued to act on stage, in television and films. Since then he has written: *Good Times/Bad Times* (novel), *P.S. Your Cat is Dead!* (Play and novel), *American Grotesque* (novel), *U.T.B.U*, (Unhealthy To Be Unpleasant - play), and he is the co-author of the book of *A Chorus Line*, (the Broadway musical, not the film) which won for him the Pulitzer Prize and a Tony Award.

OTHER TITLES AVAILABLE FROM SAMUEL FRENCH

TAKE HER, SHE'S MINE
Phoebe and Henry Ephron

Comedy / 11m, 6f / Various Sets
Art Carney and Phyllis Thaxter played the Broadway roles of parents of two typical American girls enroute to college. The story is based on the wild and wooly experiences the authors had with their daughters, Nora Ephron and Delia Ephron, themselves now well known writers. The phases of a girl's life are cause for enjoyment except to fearful fathers. Through the first two years, the authors tell us, college girls are frightfully sophisticated about all departments of human life. Then they pass into the "liberal" period of causes and humanitarianism, and some into the intellectual lethargy of beatniksville. Finally, they start to think seriously of their lives as grown ups. It's an experience in growing up, as much for the parents as for the girls.

"A warming comedy. A delightful play about parents vs kids. It's loaded with laughs. It's going to be a smash hit."
– *New York Mirror*

SAMUELFRENCH.COM

OTHER TITLES AVAILABLE FROM SAMUEL FRENCH

CAPTIVE
Jan Buttram

Comedy / 2m, 1f / Interior

A hilarious take on a father/daughter relationship, this off beat comedy combines foreign intrigue with down home philosophy. Sally Pound flees a bad marriage in New York and arrives at her parent's home in Texas hoping to borrow money from her brother to pay a debt to gangsters incurred by her husband. Her elderly parents are supposed to be vacationing in Israel, but she is greeted with a shotgun aimed by her irascible father who has been left home because of a minor car accident and is not at all happy to see her. When a news report indicates that Sally's mother may have been taken captive in the Middle East, Sally's hard-nosed brother insists that she keep father home until they receive definite word, and only then will he loan Sally the money. Sally fails to keep father in the dark, and he plans a rescue while she finds she is increasingly unable to skirt the painful truths of her life. The ornery father and his loveable but slightly-dysfunctional daughter come to a meeting of hearts and minds and solve both their problems.

SAMUELFRENCH.COM

OTHER TITLES AVAILABLE FROM SAMUEL FRENCH

COCKEYED
William Missouri Downs

Comedy / 3m, 1f / Unit Set

Phil, an average nice guy, is madly in love with the beautiful Sophia. The only problem is that she's unaware of his existence. He tries to introduce himself but she looks right through him. When Phil discovers Sophia has a glass eye, he thinks that might be the problem, but soon realizes that she really can't see him. Perhaps he is caught in a philosophical hyperspace or dualistic reality or perhaps beautiful women are just unaware of nice guys. Armed only with a B.A. in philosophy, Phil sets out to prove his existence and win Sophia's heart. This fast moving farce is the winner of the HotCity Theatre's GreenHouse New Play Festival. The St. Louis Post-Dispatch called Cockeyed a clever romantic comedy, Talkin' Broadway called it "hilarious," while Playback Magazine said that it was "fresh and invigorating."

**Winner!
of the HotCity Theatre GreenHouse New Play Festival**

"Rocking with laughter...hilarious...polished and engaging work draws heavily on the age-old conventions of farce: improbable situations, exaggerated characters, amazing coincidences, absurd misunderstandings, people hiding in closets and barely missing each other as they run in and out of doors...full of comic momentum as Cockeyed hurtles toward its conclusion."
–Talkin' Broadway

SAMUELFRENCH.COM

OTHER TITLES AVAILABLE FROM SAMUEL FRENCH

MURDER AMONG FRIENDS
Bob Barry

Comedy thriller / 4m, 2f / Interior

Take an aging, exceedingly vain actor; his very rich wife; a double dealing, double loving agent, plunk them down in an elegant New York duplex and add dialogue crackling with wit and laughs, and you have the basic elements for an evening of pure, sophisticated entertainment. Angela, the wife and Ted, the agent, are lovers and plan to murder Palmer, the actor, during a contrived robbery on New Year's Eve. But actor and agent are also lovers and have an identical plan to do in the wife. A murder occurs, but not one of the planned ones.

"Clever, amusing, and very surprising."
– *New York Times*

"A slick, sophisticated show that is modern and very funny."
– WABC TV

SAMUELFRENCH.COM

www.ingramcontent.com/pod-product-compliance
Lightning Source LLC
Chambersburg PA
CBHW070644300426
44111CB00013B/2256